Kaplan Books Relating to Law School Admissions

Getting into Law School 1998
LSAT 1997–98
Two Real LSATS Explained

Other Books in This Series

The Insider's Book of Business School Lists
The Insider's Book of Medical School Lists

THE INSIDER'S BOOK OF LAW SCHOOL LISTS

by Mark Baker

Simon & Schuster

Kaplan Books
Published by Kaplan Educational Centers and Simon & Schuster
1230 Avenue of the Americas
New York, NY 10020

Copyright © 1997 by Kaplan Educational Centers

All rights reserved. No part of this book may be reproduced or transmitted in any form or by any means, electronic or mechanical, including photocopying, recording, or by any information storage and retrieval system, without the written permission of the Publisher, except where permitted by law.

Kaplan® is a registered trademark of Kaplan Educational Centers.

Manufactured in the United States of America
Published Simultaneously in Canada

August 1997

10 9 8 7 6 5 4 3 2 1

The data in this book is subject to frequent change. Every attempt was made to ensure that all figures were current at the time this book went to press.

The author thanks Frank Fortunato, Robyn English Turner, and Ron Green for their research, wit, and gracious cooperation; and Lee Rinaldo of Sonic Youth and Joe Woodard for their expert input on music and culture.

Special thanks are extended to Linda Volpano, Sara Pearl, and Trent Anderson.

Project Editor: Richard Christiano
Production Coordinator: Gerard Capistrano
Production Editor: Maude Spekes
Cover Design: Amy McHenry
Text Design/Production: gumption design
Assistant Managing Editor: Brent Gallenberger
Managing Editor: Kiernan McGuire
Executive Editor: Del Franz

ISSN: 1093-1422
ISBN: 0-684-84177-0

CONTENTS

INTRODUCTION 1

PART ONE: GETTING IN AND STAYING IN 3
Least Expensive Tuition 5
Most Expensive Tuition 7
LSAT Scores 8
For Those Who Hated School . . . Until Now 10
For Those Who Can't Take Rejection 11
For Snob Appeal 13
Big Fish, Small Pond 13
Anonymity is the Best Defense .14
For Travel Bugs 15
For the Suits 17
For the Idealists 19
Crime and Punishment 20
Ambulance Chaser, Heal Thyself 21
Save the Whales School of Law .22
D-I-V-O-R-C-E 23
007 With A License to Sue 24
Never Forget Sabotage 25
Where You Can Kick Yourself
   For Being A Lawyer 26
Where You Can Learn to Repair
   the Damage You'll Do 27
If Your Favorite National Holiday is April 15 28
For Robocop 29
On the Side of the Human Race 30
For the Shrink-Solicitor 31
If You Believe in the Power of Prayer 31
For Those Who Really Just Want to Run for President . . .32
Mano a Mano 34
Safety in Numbers 35

Rug Rats Welcome 36
Especially for Bookworms 38
Virtual Virtual Reality 40
States with the Most Law Schools 41
One-Horse Towns 46

PART TWO: LIFESTYLE 47
Most Eligible Men 49
Most Eligible Women 50
For the Old Fogies 51
For the Young And the Restless 52
Cultural Diversity 52
Most Exotic Student Body 53
Schools with Women as Faculty 54
For the Open-Minded 55
Schools for Arch Conservatives 56
Lowest Unemployment 60
Schools in the Sticks 64
Big City Schools 65
Suburbia, Here I Come 68
Crime Rates By Region 69
Good Cops, Bad Cops 73
Most Annual Precipitation 77
The Good, the Not-So-Bad, and the Ugly 80

PART THREE: ENTERTAINMENT VALUE 85
Near the Beach 87
Near Great Skiing 92
Near Great Zoos and Aquariums 93
Near Great Roller Coasters 96
Near Great Malls 98
Near Natural Wonders 101
Near Great Microbreweries 105
Schools Near Sour Mash Bourbon Distilleries 113
In Wine Country 114
Near Great Tennis 117
Near Great Baseball 119

Near Great Horse Racing 122
Near Great Football 125
Near Great Hockey 127
Near Legalized Gambling 128
Near Great Basketball 132
Near Great Golf 134
Near Great Stock-Car Racing 136
Near Great Museums 140
Near Great Classical Music 144
Near Rock and Roll Legends 149
Near Great Country And Western Music 151
On the Lollapalooza Tour 152
Near the Alternative Rock Scene 155
Must-See Films For Lawyers 157
Lawyer Jokes 159

PART FOUR: YOUR FUTURE 161
Highest Rate of Job Placement 162
Highest Average Starting Salaries 164
Graduates Who Are Bestselling Authors 165
Graduates on the Supreme Court 167
Graduated Members of the O. J. Nightmare Team 168
Where the Living Is Easy 170
Near the Jobs 173
Just in Case 175

INTRODUCTION

So you've made it through 12 years of basic education, at least four years of college, and now you're on the verge of mortgaging the ranch for three more years of textbooks, lectures, all-nighters banging out term papers, and weekends in the library instead of on the beach. By continuing your studies in law school, you've committed yourself to one of the most demanding, stressful, pressurized lifestyles in America today, perhaps rivaled only by deep-sea diving underwater welders and air traffic controllers. Right now it looks like a long, hard road rolling out in front of you toward infinity. You've probably narrowed your choices down to three or four schools that fit your credentials, your special talents, and your budget. If you're like most law school candidates, you've filled out a mountain of forms. You've spent countless hours polishing and updating your personal essay, trying to walk that incredibly thin line between sucking up and stuck up. Then there's the begging for letters of recommendation and the awful fear that some professor or employer is suddenly going to go psycho on you and have you blackballed globally.

What you want most—more than another Cross pen and pencil set—is just a little break from the pressure cooker: a change of perspective, a couple of laughs. That's where *The Insider's Book of Law School Lists* comes in.

These lists put the next few years of grueling higher education into a broader, more worldly context. There's more to life than going to class. What about surfing, shopping, and rock-and-roll? What about the ratio of days of sunshine to days of rain? What about roller coasters, golf, and stock-car racing? And there's more to education than just lectures, projects, and tests. What about great overseas study programs, cheap-o application fees, famous and infamous alumni, and flexible classroom hours? Which schools have the most eligible women, and which have the most eligible men?

We would never suggest that you make a final decision about which institution of higher learning to set your heart upon simply by referring to our list of schools on the Lollapalooza tour. It wouldn't be right to decide to attend a law school just because it was located within 30 minutes of great skiing. No one in his right mind would pick a law school just because it was near some of the best microbreweries in the nation. Right?

On the other hand, these details of life and education are not to be sniffed at. You've worked really hard to get where you are today—teetering on the brink of three more years of even harder work—so maybe it wouldn't be such a bad idea to include the Fun Factor in your equation for the perfect law school. Passion in life is a good thing. So what if your passion is for mall crawling and lounge lizards? If you're going to do your best in law school, you need an outlet for your extracurricular passions and you've got to keep in touch with real life beyond the halls of academe. In short, you need a school that will help you claw your way to the top instead of ripping you to shreds.

A few of the lists compiled in the following pages are strictly serious, some are seriously silly, and a few are strictly for laughs. I have a feeling you could use a good laugh about now. So plow right in and read cover to cover, or use the table of contents to choose the subjects you want to investigate further or the schools you'd like to know more about. However you choose to absorb this essential information about your future, be sure to relax and enjoy yourself.

GETTING IN AND STAYING IN

"During my teaching days, I began the study of the law. I am not sure what influenced me to make this choice. I knew that I never intended to work with my hands, and no doubt I was attracted by the show of the legal profession. When I was still quite young, the lawyers from the county seat always visited our town on all public occasions. On the Fourth of July and on Decoration Day, in political campaigns, and on all holidays, they made speeches and were altogether the most conspicuous of the locality. . . . I enjoyed the way the pettifoggers abused each other, and as I grew toward maturity, I developed a desire to be a lawyer, too . . . .

"When I considered I was ready for the test, I presented myself, with some dozen other ambitious young men, for the examination. A committee of lawyers was appointed to try us out. That committee did not seem to take it as seriously as examiners do today. I was not made to feel that the safety of the government or the destiny of the universe was hanging on their verdict. As I remember it now, the whole class was passed, and I became a member of the Ohio Bar.

"My neighbors and friends warmly congratulated me, but it was some time before they encouraged me with any employment. They could not conceive that a boy whom they knew and who was brought up in their town could possibly have the ability and learning that they thought was necessary to the practice of the law."

—Clarence Darrow
The Story of My Life
originally published in 1932
DeCapo Press Edition, 1996

Getting In and Staying In

There are plenty of theories about how to choose the best law school. There's the Academic Theory, which insists that the toughest school with the highest academic standards is the only logical choice. There's the Status Theory, which posits that your future will be assured only if you attend a law school with a national reputation for snooty social credentials. If you subscribe to the You Get What You Pay For theory, then only the most expensive law school will do. Those are only a few of the more prominent theories.

The Insider's Book of Law School Lists just doesn't buy any of them. They all have their place, and perhaps some merit. But they all concentrate on the schools and leave you, the prospective student, out of the equation. If you're going to do your best in law school, and you want an institution that will nurture your success, fulfill your dreams, and guarantee your future, then the first thing to decide is what you want—your likes and dislikes, your strengths and foibles.

Just for a change, let's concentrate on what will make you happy. What sort of working conditions will make you comfortable? How much are you willing to pay? What kind of a crowd will you be hanging with in this joint? There's no reason to spend all that money, work up all that mental sweat, and suffer the fear of failure if the place where you're trying to claw out a law degree just isn't you. Some people like professors breathing down their necks: They think plastic pocket protectors are a fashion statement and nothing makes them happier than tuition payments just slightly lower than the national debt. Maybe you're one of those people, and maybe you're not. This first chapter will help you find out for sure, and provide some guideposts to the academic institu-

> "Courage is the most important attribute of a lawyer. It is more important than competence or vision. It can never be an elective in any law school. It can never be delimited, dated, or outworn, and it should pervade the heart, the halls of justice, and the chambers of the mind."
>
> —Robert F. Kennedy, 1962

tion that is right for you in terms of tuition, facilities, special programs, and peer groups.

Choosing a law school should be exciting, never intimidating. You should be pumped and raring to go. With the help of this book, picking a law school should feel like the exhilaration of extreme sports instead of just more homework. So hook yourself up and stand in the door. This is the jumping-off place—Geronimo!

LEAST EXPENSIVE TUITION

Bargain-basement tuition is almost always available only at state colleges and universities, and even then is exclusively available for residents of the state. Out-of-state students pay a premium. But the price at these institutions is at least $15,000 cheaper than the name-brand private schools. That kind of money could defray the costs of relocation, and of sitting around for the six months to a year it takes to gain residency, not to mention cutting down on your future loan payments.

The schools in the following list charge under $5,000 per year for in-state tuition, and under $10,000 per year for out-of-state tuition. North Carolina Central University School of Law has the least expensive in-state tuition; University of Arkansas at Little Rock School of Law has the least expensive out-of-state tuition.

Under $3,000

		Resident	Out-of-State
1.	North Carolina Central University School of Law	$1,890	$10,842
2.	Georgia State University College of Law	$2,903	$9,147

Under $4,000

1.	University of Mississippi School of Law	$3,081	$7,003
2.	Southern University Law Center	$3,088	$6,288

3. University of New Mexico School of Law	$3,283	$11,015
4. University of Idaho	$3,308	$8,960
5. University of Georgia School of Law	$3,315	$10,017
6. University of Arkansas at Fayetteville School of Law	$3,363	$7,275
7. University of Alabama School of Law	$3,578	$7,712
8. Florida State University College of Law	$3,687	$11,583
9. University of Tennessee College of Law	$3,794	$9,620
10. University of Memphis, Cecil C. Humphreys School of Law	$3,852	$9,680
11. University of Arkansas at Little Rock School of Law	$3,891	$8,597
12. University of Wyoming	$3,920	$8,648
13. Louisiana State University, Paul M. Hebert Law Center	$3,936	$8,556
14. University of North Dakota School of Law	$3,948	$8,174
15. University of Nebraska College of Law	$3,953	$8,535

Under $5,000

1. University of Arizona College of Law	$4,010	$10,378
2. University of Oklahoma College of Law	$4,141	$11,779
3. University of Utah College of Law	$4,291	$9,587
4. Texas Southern University, Thurgood Marshall School of Law	$4,440	$8,080
5. Brigham Young University, J. Reuben Clark Law School	$4,780	$7,160

MOST EXPENSIVE TUITION

Here's some bad news. Not only must you have a potload of money to attend these schools, but they also require that you have great grades, an outstanding record, solid references, and a high tolerance for rejection (they get lots of applicants even at these prices). These schools have tuitions exceeding $20,000 per year (tuition is the same both in-state and out-of-state, with the exception of the last two schools on the list, which are just for out-of-state students). Out-of-state tuitions are marked with an asterisk.

1. Columbia University School of Law — $24,342
2. New York University School of Law — $24,191
3. Stanford University School of Law — $23,360
4. University of Pennsylvania Law School — $23,314
5. University of Chicago Law School — $22,755
6. Yale University, Yale Law School — $22,692
7. University of Michigan School of Law — $22,698*
8. University of Southern California Law School — $22,620
9. Georgetown University Law Center — $22,430
10. Duke University School of Law — $22,414
11. Harvard University Law School — $22,354
12. Cornell University Law School — $22,100
13. Tulane University School of Law — $22,076
14. University of Connecticut School of Law — $21,938*
15. Fordham University School of Law — $21,694
16. Catholic University of America, Columbus School of Law — $21,468
17. Northwestern University School of Law — $21,316
18. Boston College Law School — $21,290
19. University of Miami School of Law — $21,160

20. Pepperdine University School of Law	$20,900
21. Emory University School of Law	$20,890
22. Boston University School of Law	$20,834
23. Ohio Northern University, Claude W. Pettit College of Law	$20,510
24. Washington University School of Law	$20,390

LSAT SCORES

At the schools in the first list below, the median LSAT score is at least 165. At Yale University Law School and University of Chicago Law School, you'll need an LSAT score of at least 170. Obviously, this is not good news for everyone. In order to keep the tears and hair tearing to a minimum, the second list below identifies schools with a much more reasonable attitude toward test scores.

Highest Scores

1. Yale University Yale Law School	175
2. University of Chicago Law School	173
3. Columbia University School of Law	171
3. Stanford University School of Law	171
5. Duke University School of Law	170
5. New York University School of Law	170
5. University of California, Berkeley Boalt Hall School of Law	170
5. University of Michigan School of Law	170
9. Georgetown University Law Center	169
9. University of Virginia School of Law	169
11. University of Pennsylvania Law School	167
12. Cornell University Law School	166

More Reasonable Scores (Schools with Median LSAT Scores of 155 or Less)

1.	District of Columbia School of Law	147
1.	Southern University Law Center	147
3.	Thomas M. Cooley Law School	148
4.	St. Thomas University School of Law	150
4.	Texas Wesleyan University School of Law	150
6.	Widener University School of Law	151
6.	Roger Williams University School of Law	151
6.	Nova Southeastern University, Shepard Broad Law Center	151
9.	Ohio Northern University College of Law	152
10.	Western New England School of Law	153
10.	Capital University Law School	153
10.	Touro College, Jacob D. Fuchsberg Law Center	153
10.	John Marshall School of Law	153
10.	Quinnipiac College School of Law	153
15.	Syracuse University College of Law	154
15.	North Carolina Central University School of Law	154
17.	University of Tulsa College of Law	155
17.	University of Detroit Mercy School of Law	155

FOR THOSE WHO HATED SCHOOL... UNTIL NOW

Schools whose Incoming Classes Average a 3.0 GPA or Lower

Not everybody is in love with academics. The majority of people merely put up with education, and there is a certain segment of the student population that just hates school. That doesn't mean they won't do well in law school; it just means they may not have been intellectually stimulated until now, or that they haven't really applied themselves until now, or that they didn't much care what their grades were... until now. Underachievers deserve a break, too. Here are some schools where grades aren't everything. The GPA accepted for the bottom 25 percent of the entering class is hovering around 3.0 or lower.

1.	District of Columbia School of Law	2.36
2.	Southern University Law Center	2.43
3.	Quinnipiac College School of Law	2.50
4.	St. Thomas University School of Law	2.37
5.	Thomas M. Cooley Law School	2.56
6.	St. Mary's University School of Law	2.58
7.	Texas Wesleyan University School of Law	2.59
8.	North Carolina Central University School of Law	2.60
9.	Whittier Law School	2.65
10.	Northern Illinois University College of Law	2.67
10.	Nova Southeastern University Shepard Broad Law Center	2.67
12.	Franklin Pierce Law Center	2.69
12.	South Texas College of Law	2.69
12.	Touro College Jacob D. Fuchsberg Law Center	2.69
15.	Gonzaga University School of Law	2.70
15.	Howard University School of Law	2.70

17. Western New England College School of Law   2.71
17. St. John's University School of Law   2.71
19. Southwestern University School of Law   2.72
20. Michigan State University, Detroit College of Law   2.74
21. Widener University School of Law   2.75
22. Capital University Law School   2.76

FOR THOSE WHO CAN'T TAKE REJECTION

Schools That Accept 50 Percent or More of their Applicants

Nobody likes to be turned down. Rejection kicks in when you reach the age of 13, and then it never stops. If you can't stand being told to take a hike, consider attending a school with a record of accepting a high percentage of the people who apply. The schools below say "yes" to 50 percent or more of their applicants.

1. University of Vermont School of Law   78%
1. Vermont Law School   78%
3. Suffolk University School of Law   71%
3. Illinois Institute of Technology   71%
5. Capital University Law School   70%
5. Valparaiso University School of Law   70%
5. Widener University School of Law   70%
8. Albany Law School of Union University   67%
8. Thomas Jefferson School of Law   67%
8. Gonzaga University School of Law   67%
8. William Mitchell College of Law   67%
12. University of Tulsa School of Law   65%
12. Michigan State University, Detroit College of Law   65%
12. Creighton University School of Law   65%

12. Detroit College of Law at Michigan State University   65%
12. New England School of Law   65%
12. University of Missouri, Columbia, School of Law   65%
18. California Western School of Law   64%
18. Mississippi College School of Law   64%
18. Ohio Northern University, Claude W. Pettit College of Law   64%
18. University of Missouri, Kansas City, School of Law   64%
18. University of Pittsburgh School of Law   64%
18. University of Toledo College of Law   64%
24. Case Western Reserve University School of Law   63%
24. University of Detroit, Mercy School of Law   63%
26. University of Miami School of Law   62%
27. Duquesne University School of Law   61%
27. Roger Williams University School of Law   61%
27. Syracuse University School of Law   61%
27. University of South Dakota School of Law   61%
27. Western New England College School of Law   61%
32. Loyola University, New Orleans, School of Law   60%
33. Villanova University School of Law   55%
33. University of the Pacific McGeorge School of Law   55%

FOR SNOB APPEAL

Schools That Accept 20 Percent of Their Applicants or Less

So you've got great grades, a good record, outstanding references, and will get into just about any law school you want to attend? Then pick a school that's picky. Exclusivity is a good thing as long as you're not part of the crowd being excluded. The Marine Corps does it: "We're looking for a few good men." Go for the snob appeal. These schools accept 20 percent or less of the students who apply to them.

1.	Yale University Yale Law School	7%
2.	Stanford University School of Law	12%
3.	Harvard University Law School	13%
4.	Southern University School of Law	18%
4.	University of California, Berkeley Boalt Hall School of Law	18%
6.	North Carolina Central University School of Law	19%
7.	Columbia University School of Law	20%

BIG FISH, SMALL POND

Schools with Enrollments of Fewer than 400

Do you like to stand out in a crowd? Would you flourish in a more intimate environment, with a few well chosen colleagues, a hand-picked peer group of, say, 400 people or fewer? The following schools have the smallest enrollments. Be a Big Man or Woman on Campus—especially at the University of South Dakota School of Law. The following schools have an enrollment of 300 students or fewer.

1.	Thomas Cooley Law School	154
2.	Thomas Jefferson School of Law	183
3.	University of North Dakota School of Law	202

4.	Northern Kentucky University School of Law	210
5.	University of Wyoming School of Law	211
6.	University of South Dakota School of Law	213
7.	District of Columbia School of Law	226
8.	University of Hawaii School of Law	228
9.	University of Montana School of Law	230
10.	North Carolina Central University School of Law	243
11.	University of Arkansas School of Law, Little Rock	263
12.	University of Idaho School of Law	266
13.	University of Maine School of Law	284
14.	Roger Williams University School of Law	286

ANONYMITY IS THE BEST DEFENSE

Schools With Enrollments of Over 1,400

Many people find safety in numbers, others call it an opportunity for a party. If you don't want to be the lead lemming, and would rather keep your head down and hide in the herd, then schools with mega-enrollments might be your kind of place. The same goes for you party animals and social butterflies who thrive on a constant parade of people and personalities. Live large. Go to a school where you can make lots of friends and influence lots of people.

1.	Harvard University School of Law	1,646
2.	Georgetown University Law Center	1,626
3.	University of Texas School of Law, Austin	1,542
4.	New York University School of Law	1,342
5.	University of California School of Law, Hastings	1,292
6.	George Washington University, the National Law Center	1,284
7.	University of Virginia School of Law	1,148

8. University of Miami School of Law   1,125
9. University of Florida School of Law   1,104
10. Columbia University School of Law   1,073
11. University of Michigan School of Law   1,068
12. Boston University School of Law   1.064
13. Fordham University School of Law   1,043
14. Suffolk University School of Law   1,010

FOR TRAVEL BUGS

Schools with Study-Abroad Programs

What a concept! You go to law school and get to live in an exotic foreign locale at the same time. As long as your overseas study program is approved by the American Bar Association, you can still wander back to the States at the end and keep your credits. Better yet, go native—many programs prepare you to practice in the host country. There are over 100 ABA-approved programs offered through a variety of American law schools. Here are the ones that had their own Web sites at the time this book was published.

Temple University School of Law

Summer session in Tel Aviv, Israel. This program has a longstanding reputation of excellence. ABA site evaluation report calls it "outstanding" and a "model summer program." Visit their Web site at: http://www.temple.edu/lawschool/telaviv.html

Duke University School of Law

Summer program in Hong Kong. This program is designed especially for students planning a career in transactional law in Asia and the Pacific Rim and for foreign students who plan to study in the United States. Visit their Web site at:
http://www.law.duke.edu/internat/hkg/asiatofc.html

William and Mary University

Summer program in Adelaide, Australia. This is a law program in conjunction with the University of Adelaide (UA) in South Australia. UA has an international reputation for teaching and research. This program utilizes the court and government agencies located in the capital city. Visit their Web site at:
http://warthog.cc.wm.edu/law/sumlaw/austral.htm

Case Western Reserve University School of Law and Cleveland State University, Cleveland-Marshal College of Law

St. Petersburg, Russia. This one-month summer program is from the joint Russian Legal Studies Program of CWRU and CSU (ABA approved) at the St. Petersburg Summer Law Institute (ABA approved) in Russia. Visit their Web site at:
http://lawwww.cwru.edu/summerlaw/index.html

University of Detroit Year in London Program

Offers course work that is ABA approved. The program is flexible in that you can take American law courses in London to fill graduation requirements.

University of Houston

Mexico City, Mexico. Since this program was established in 1968, it has trained hundreds of American lawyers in Mexican law and legal relations between Mexico and the United States. Many alums are now practicing law in Mexico. Visit their Web site at:
http://www.law.uh.edu/lawcenter/programs/mlsp/mexican.html

FOR THE SUITS
Schools with Programs in Business Law

For those of you who really enjoy evicting widows and orphans, or who would love to defend some fabulously wealthy stock manipulator, or who know that the best way to get rich is to hang out with people who make money, a law school that offers a program in business law would be best.

Boston College Law School

Boston University School of Law

Brigham Young University Law School

Brooklyn Law School

Capital University Law School

Case Western Reserve University School of Law

Catholic University of America, Columbus School of Law

College of William and Mary School of Law

Cornell University Law School

Duke University School of Law

Fordham University School of Law

Georgetown University Law Center

George Washington University Law School

Harvard University Law School

Indiana University School of Law

Mercer University School of Law

New York University School of Law

Ohio Northern University College of Law

Oklahoma University School of Law

Rutgers, The State University of New Jersey School of Law

Samford University, Cumberland School of Law

Southern Methodist University School of Law

Southwestern University School of Law

Stanford Law School

Stetson University College of Law

Suffolk University Law School

Temple University School of Law

Tulane University Law School

University of Akron School of Law

University of Arizona College of Law

University of Baltimore School of Law

University of California, Hastings College of Law

University of California at Los Angeles

University of Dayton School of Law

University of Iowa College of Law

University of Kansas School of Law

University of Kentucky College of Law

University of Minnesota Law School

University of North Carolina School of Law

University of Oklahoma College of Law

University of Pennsylvania Law School

University of Pittsburgh School of Law

University of San Diego School of Law

University of South Carolina School of Law

University of Southern California Law Center

University of Tennessee College of Law

University of Texas School of Law

University of Utah College of Law

University of Washington School of Law

Vanderbilt University School of Law

Wake Forest University School of Law

Washington and Lee University School of Law

Washington University School of Law

Western New England College School of Law

Widener University School of Law

William Mitchell College of Law

FOR THE IDEALISTS
Schools with Programs in Public Policy

Starting salaries for recent law grads in public-interest positions are only about $25,000 a year. Only two percent of all law school graduates begin their careers practicing law in the public interest. Because of rising tuition rates in private law schools, many are beginning to establish loan forgiveness programs to encourage graduates to pursue low-paying, public-interest jobs. If you really want a thankless job that pays next to nothing, then choose a law school with a program in public policy.

Northern Illinois University College of Law

Northeastern University School of Law

Hamline University School of Law

Nova Southeastern University, Shephard Broad Law Center

City University of New York School of Law

Golden Gate University School of Law

Detroit College of Law, Michigan State University

University of Akron School of Law

University of Wyoming College of Law

Lewis & Clark College, Northwestern School of Law

CRIME AND PUNISHMENT

Schools with Programs in Criminal Law

Bad boys, bad boys! Whatcha gonna do when they come for you? Usually, the bad boys call an attorney. If you don't mind the institutional green paint they use in almost every jail in America, attend a law school with a good program in criminal law. Just remember, the cops will hate your guts whether you prosecute or defend, so don't do it if you just want to hang out with guys in uniform.

Boston College Law School

Boston University School of Law

Brigham Young University Law School

Brooklyn Law School

Capital University Law School

Columbia University School of Law

Duke University School of Law

Fordham University School of Law

George Washington University Law School

Harvard University Law School

Indiana University School of Law

New York University School of Law

Ohio Northern University College of Law

Oklahoma City University School of Law

Southwestern University School of Law

Stetson University College of Law

Temple University School of Law

University of Akron School of Law

University of Baltimore School of Law

University of California, Hastings College of Law

University of California at Los Angeles

University of Dayton School of Law

University of Kansas School of Law

University of North Carolina School of Law

University of Pittsburgh School of Law

University of San Diego School of Law

University of Washington School of Law

Vanderbilt University School of Law

Washington and Lee University School of Law

Western New England College School of Law

Widener University School of Law

William Mitchell College of Law

AMBULANCE CHASER, HEAL THYSELF
Schools Combining Law and Health-Related Issues

The following schools offer programs combining law and health related issues: medical malpractice is the first big issue that comes to mind. Doctors make great clients. If you're defending them, they have great insurance policies, so you're sure to get paid. If the patient is your plaintiff, your payday is likely in the bag, since juries have been whacking away at physicians in the last 10 years. This is a win-win situation for the right lawyer.

Boston University School of Law

George Washington University Law School

Georgetown University Law Center

Samford University, Cumberland School of Law

Tulane University Law School

University of Houston Law Center

University of Iowa College of Law

University of Kansas School of Law

University of Michigan Law School

University of North Carolina School of Law

University of Oklahoma College of Law

University of Pittsburgh School of Law

University of Washington School of Law

Washington University School of Law

SAVE THE WHALES SCHOOL OF LAW
Schools with Programs in Environmental Law

If you are truly serious about protecting tiny fish, slimy snails, spotted owls, and other cuddly endangered species, then choose a law school that emphasizes environmental issues. The proliferation of local, state, and federal laws to protect the air, water, wildlife, and virgin forests has provided new battlegrounds for lawyers all across the nation. Idealists, beware: You're more likely to find yourself arranging swaps of pollution licenses for restored wetlands, not plugging the hole in the ozone layer.

Boston University School of Law

Duke University School of Law

Indiana University School of Law

Samford University, Cumberland School of Law

University of Michigan Law School

University of Oklahoma College of Law

University of Washington School of Law

Yale University, Yale Law School

D-I-V-O-R-C-E

Schools with Programs in Family Law

With a third of all American marriages ending in divorce, family law would seem to be a good specialty to study. It's a messy job, but somebody's got to do it. There is one serious occupational hazard: After hearing all those stories about infidelity, it's tough to believe your spouse's excuses about working late at the office.

Boston College Law School

Brigham Young University Law School

New York University School of Law

Oklahoma City University School of Law

Southwestern University School of Law

Stetson University College of Law

Suffolk University Law School

Temple University School of Law

University of Arizona College of Law

University of Baltimore School of Law

University of California, Hastings College of Law

University of Kansas School of Law

University of Minnesota Law School

University of Oklahoma College of Law

University of Pittsburgh School of Law

University of Southern California Law Center

Western New England College School of Law

William Mitchell College of Law

007 WITH A LICENSE TO SUE

Schools with Courses in International Law

International law—it conjures up images of speeding along in an Aston Martin on the winding roads above Monte Carlo or Cannes, yachting in the Mediterranean Sea, and dining at black tie affairs in Kuala Lumpur. The truth is that the real opportunities in international law are now opening up in the dull, gray capital cities of formerly communist countries—Russia and its former satellites in eastern Europe. The real world class power, currently flexing its dragonlike economic, military, and population muscles, is China, where they put the defendant and his lawyer in prison before the trial. Learn Chinese and experiment with living on cockroaches, just in case.

Boston University School of Law

Columbia University School of Law

Florida State University College of Law

George Washington University Law School

Stanford University Law School

University of Chicago School of Law

University of Denver College of Law

University of Michigan Law School

University of Pittsburgh School of Law

University of San Diego School of Law

University of Southern California Law Center

University of Washington School of Law

NEVER FORGET SABOTAGE

Schools with Programs Concentrating on Labor Law

That phrase was one of the more radical slogans of the American trade union, the Industrial Workers of the World (IWW), popularly known as the Wobblies. They began a tradition of linking lawyers and labor back in the early 1900s, when industrialists could still sue unions for conspiracy to block trade, and employers would often force workers to sign yellow dog contracts, swearing that they would not join a union. Leaders of the IWW were always in jail; in fact, Joe Hill was convicted of murder and executed.

This tradition continued into the modern era of labor unions: Jimmy Hoffa was tried and convicted of jury tampering, mail fraud, and mishandling of union funds, and United Mine Workers president Tony Boyle was tried for conspiracy in the murder of one of his rivals. Whether you're keeping them out of jail or negotiating their newest contracts, specializing in labor related law can be a remunerative field—as long as you don't try on the cement shoes.

The following schools have programs concentrating on labor law. The only odd thing is that none of these programs are in Chicago, the big-shouldered home of the labor movement in America.

Boston College Law School

Capital University Law School

Columbia University School of Law

Fordham University School of Law

Mercer University School of Law

New York University School of Law

Oklahoma City University School of Law

Rutgers, The State University of New Jersey School of Law

Southwestern University School of Law

University of Akron School of Law

University of Minnesota Law School

University of Pennsylvania Law School

University of Pittsburgh School of Law

University of San Diego School of Law

University of Tennessee College of Law

West Virginia University College of Law

Western New England College School of Law

William Mitchell College of Law

WHERE YOU CAN KICK YOURSELF FOR BEING A LAWYER

Schools with Joint Degrees in Law and Philosophy

It's not easy living in the looking-glass world of advocacy. One day you're throwing the switch on the electric chair, the next day you find yourself defending a murderer. Many people lose their moral moorings in a habitat where words, laws, and lives can be bent and twisted into unrecognizable shapes. Truth becomes lies, and vice versa. It's tricky hanging on to your scruples being a lawyer, so it wouldn't hurt to have a firm grounding in philosophy—especially in existentialism and situation ethics. These schools offer joint degrees in law and philosophy.

Catholic University of America, Columbus School of Law

Columbia University School of Law

Georgetown University Law Center

Rutgers, The State University of New Jersey School of Law

State University of New York, Buffalo School of Law

University of Arizona College of Law

University of Kansas School of Law

University of Pennsylvania Law School

University of Southern California Law Center

University of Washington School of Law

WHERE YOU CAN LEARN TO REPAIR THE DAMAGE YOU'LL DO
Schools That Offer Joint Degrees in Law and Social Work

You're going to catch a lot of flak about being a lawyer. People will accuse you of all sorts of flagrant sins against humanity. Lawyers are held up to ridicule and scorned for their lack of concern for their fellow man and woman. You'll be blamed for the breakdown of the nuclear family, civility, the social contract, the bonds of brother- and sisterhood . . . and father- and motherhood, for that matter. The best defense is a good offense: Get yourself a joint degree in social work. When you win your case and the opposition calls you a heartless fiend who doesn't care about anybody's feelings, you can flip out your parchment and rebut with, "Oh, yeah? Read it and weep."

Boston College Law School

Case Western Reserve University School of Law

Catholic University of America, Columbus School of Law

Columbia University School of Law

New York University Law School

State University of New York, Buffalo School of Law

University of Denver College of Law

University of Kansas School of Law

University of Pennsylvania Law School

University of Southern California Law Center

University of Washington School of Law

Washington University School of Law

IF YOUR FAVORITE NATIONAL HOLIDAY IS APRIL 15

Schools with Programs in Taxation

There are definitely some advantages to specializing in taxation. You and the funeral director will never go out of business. People might not want to talk to you very often, but when they need you, they really need you—and the more creative you are, the better. If you should actually take the radical step of working for the IRS, you'll be able to make just about anybody—no matter what his station in life, income, or fame—shake in his boots and eat his liver. That's real power. However, people will tend to move away from you when you sit down in your local bar, and your marital choices will be severely limited to federal employees only. But it's your choice. Here's the list of schools offering an LL.M. in taxation.

Arizona State University College of Law

Boston University School of Law

California Western School of Law

Catholic University of America, Columbus School of Law

Chicago-Kent College of Law

Columbia University School of Law

Franklin Pierce Law Center

George Mason University School of Law

George Washington University National Law Center

Golden Gate University School of Law

John Marshall School of Law

New York Law School

Stanford University Law School

Syracuse University College of Law

University of Baltimore School of Law

University of California at Berkeley

University of Dayton School of Law

University of Georgia School of Law

University of Houston Law Center

Vanderbilt University School of Law

FOR ROBOCOP

Schools with Courses in the Relationship Between Technology and the Law

In Arthur C. Clarke's *2001: A Space Odyssey*, was HAL (the computer that killed the human astronauts traveling to Jupiter) guilty of first-degree murder or a lesser charge of manslaughter? Was he acting in self-defense, as he claimed, or was he not guilty by reason of insanity? Should the captain of the mission, who turned HAL off, be tried for violation of the rights of a sentient being? If you'd actually like to sit down and talk about this late into the night, then the future is in your hands—especially if you choose a school where you can concentrate on areas where technology and the law intersect. Here are your choices.

Arizona State University College of Law

Boston University School of Law

California Western School of Law

Catholic University of America, Columbus School of Law

Chicago-Kent College of Law

Columbia University School of Law

Franklin Pierce Law Center

George Mason University School of Law

George Washington University National Law Center

Golden Gate University School of Law

John Marshall School of Law

New York Law School

Stanford University Law School

Syracuse University College of Law

University of Baltimore School of Law

University of California at Berkeley

University of Dayton School of Law

University of Georgia School of Law

University of Houston Law Center

Vanderbilt University School of Law

ON THE SIDE OF THE HUMAN RACE

Schools with Courses in the Relationship between Human Rights and the Law

Human rights is one of the hottest topics in law today, and it's about time. This is one area in the law and our daily lives in which fairness really counts. Since we're all human, we all benefit. Plus, there are some huge awards being handed out in sexual harassment and human rights violations cases.

American University, Washington College of Law

Yeshiva University, Benjamin N. Cardozo School of Law

Columbia University School of Law

Howard University School of Law

University of Cincinnati College of Law

University of Miami School of Law

FOR THE SHRINK-SOLICITOR
Schools Offering Joint Degrees in Law and Psychology

Think how much more deeply you'll be able to delve into the criminal mind, spot your opponents' fetishes and foibles, and sway a jury of utter strangers if you know exactly how minds work. This is the obvious advantage of getting a joint degree in psychology. Another less obvious benefit is the fact that you can write a pop psychology how-to book and make a million bucks off all the head cases out there. Not a bad hedge in case this lawyer stuff doesn't pan out. This is a list of the law schools which offer joint degrees in psychology.

Brigham Young University Law School

Catholic University of America, Columbus School of Law

University of Arizona College of Law

University of Denver College of Law

University of Tulsa College of Law

University of Washington School of Law

Widener University School of Law

IF YOU BELIEVE IN THE POWER OF PRAYER
Schools Offering Joint Degrees in Law and Religion

A joint degree in law and religion can only be an asset in private practice or public service. After all, the most famous of ancient codes of law is the first five books of the Bible: The laws of Moses, an elaboration of the Ten Commandments. Think how much better prepared Henry Kissinger would have been when he found himself on his knees in the White House with President Richard Nixon if the Secretary of State had possessed a joint degree in law and religion. He would have known how to minister to his boss's spiritual needs, and he would have had the acumen to get up and run like hell when he found out what his boss had done. A thorough study of religion may be handy some day in the distant future when you finally come before the Final Judge to receive your personal thumbs up or thumbs down.

Emory University School of Law

Oklahoma City University School of Law

Samford University, Cumberland School of Law

University of Southern California Law Center

Vanderbilt University School of Law

Yale University, Yale Law School

FOR THOSE WHO REALLY JUST WANT TO RUN FOR PRESIDENT

Although there have been a few soldiers, actors, and peanut farmers elected to the highest office in the land, an awful lot of American presidents have been lawyers. In fact, politics in general is dominated by members of the bar. It's no wonder the country is so burdened down with statute law: that's one of the things lawyers do best. For all our sakes, if you do think you want to be in charge of the rest of us some day, please take the time and make the effort to prepare more than your smile and your handshake for public office. Get a joint degree in political science, public administration, or public affairs. A grateful nation thanks you.

Schools Offering Joint Degrees in Law and Political Science

Brooklyn Law School

Duke University School of Law

Georgetown University Law Center

Rutgers, The State University of New Jersey School of Law

Stanford University Law School

State University of New York at Buffalo, SUNY School of Law

University of Iowa College of Law

University of Washington School of Law

Washington University School of Law

Schools Offering Joint Degrees in Public Administration

Brigham Young University Law School

Brooklyn Law School

Catholic University of America, Columbus School of Law

Florida State University College of Law

George Washington University Law School

Georgia State University College of Law

Hamline University School of Law

Harvard University Law School

New York University School of Law

Samford University, Cumberland School of Law

Suffolk University Law School

University of Akron School of Law

University of Arizona College of Law

University of Baltimore School of Law

University of Dayton School of Law

University of Kansas School of Law

University of Kentucky College of Law

University of North Carolina at Chapel Hill School of Law

University of South Carolina School of Law

University of Southern California Law Center

University of Tennessee College of Law

University of Utah College of Law

West Virginia University College of Law

Yale University, Yale Law School

Schools Offering Joint Degrees in Law and Public Affairs

Columbia University School of Law

Indiana University at Bloomington School of Law

New York University School of Law

Southern Illinois University School of Law

Stanford University Law School

University of Minnesota Law School

University of Pittsburgh School of Law

University of Texas at Austin School of Law

University of Washington School of Law

Yale University, Yale Law School

MANO A MANO

Schools where Core Class Enrollments Are Fewer than 50

Small classes mean more individual attention, closer supervision of studies, and intense exchanges of knowledge. Professors get to know your face, your name, your strengths, and your weaknesses. Participation in class discussions is not only accessible and natural, it's impossible to avoid. If all this scares the heck out of you, then steer clear of the following schools whose core classes number 50 students or fewer. The numbers are averages.

1.	University of Kansas School of Law	20
1.	University of San Diego School of Law	20
3.	Emory University School of Law	23
4.	Washington & Lee University School of Law	26
5.	Stanford University Law School	35
5.	University of Arizona College of Law	35
5.	University of Utah College of Law	35

8.	Temple University School of Law	39
8.	William Mitchell College of Law	39
10.	Ohio Northern University College of Law	40
10.	University of Dayton School of Law	40
10.	Wake Forest University School of Law	40
13.	Northern Illinois University College of Law	42
14.	Florida State University College of Law	45
15.	University of Chicago School of Law	46
16.	Brooklyn Law School	49

SAFETY IN NUMBERS

Schools with the Largest Core Classes

There's something to be said for sleeping in a big lecture hall after a long night hitting the books or hitting the hot spots. Plus, you're paying your hard-earned bucks for the information inside those professors' heads, not to hear a bunch of amateurs spout off in "a dialogue of give and take." Let the professor lecture and let the students do what they do best. Here are the schools with the largest core classes—at least larger than 90 students.

1.	Northwestern University School of Law	100
1.	University of Iowa College of Law	100
1.	University of Texas at Austin School of Law	100
4.	Boston College Law School	98
5.	Tulane University Law School	95
5.	University of Michigan Law School	95
5.	University of Pennsylvania Law School	95
8.	Boston University School of Law	90
8.	Brigham Young University Law School	90
8.	University of Pittsburgh School of Law	90
8.	Vanderbilt University School of Law	90

RUG RATS WELCOME
Schools Offering Day Care

At first, burger flippers only had to be alive, then the franchises started insisting on high school diplomas. Today the burger joints are full of college graduates with English majors, Ph.Ds in philosophy, and former legislators. Older men and women are going back to graduate school to get their law degrees to better compete in the modern world. Many of these individuals have real lives, one or two jobs, on-going relationships with another person that last for more than two weeks; believe it or not, some of them have children. For these brave students, here is a list of law schools affiliated with universities that offer day care services. For you young single guys and gals, the answer is no, there isn't anyone to throw a Frisbee to your golden retriever while you're in class, and no one provides cat sitters to keep your new kitten from clawing up your futon while you're in school.

Arizona State University, Tempe, AZ

Baylor University, Waco, TX

Boston College, Chestnut Hill, MA

Boston University, Boston, MA

Brigham Young University, Provo, UT

City University of New York, School of Law at Queens College, New York, NY

College of William and Mary, Williamsburg, VA

Columbia University, New York, NY

Duke University, Durham, NC

Emory University, Atlanta, GA

George Mason University, Fairfax, VA

Harvard University, Cambridge, MA

Indiana University, Bloomington, IN

Louisiana State University, Shrevesport, LA

Ohio State University, Columbus, OH
Santa Clara University, Santa Clara, CA
Stanford University, Stanford, CA
State University of New York, Buffalo, NY
Syracuse University, Syracuse, NY
Tulane University, New Orleans, LA
University of Akron, Akron, OH
University of Alabama, Tuscaloosa, AL
University of California, Berkeley, CA
University of California, Davis, CA
University of Colorado, Boulder, CO
University of Detroit, Mercy, MI
University of Florida, Gainesville, FL
University of Houston, Houston, TX
University of Illinois, Chicago, IL
University of Iowa, Iowa City, IO
University of Mississippi, University, MS
University of Missouri, Columbia, MO
University of New Mexico, Albuquerque, NM
University of Notre Dame, Notre Dame, IN
University of Pennsylvania, Philadelphia, PA
University of Pittsburgh, Pittsburgh, PA
University of San Diego, San Diego, CA
University of Texas, Austin, TX
University of Washington, Seattle, WA
Washington University, St. Louis, MO
Yale University, New Haven, CT

ESPECIALLY FOR BOOKWORMS

Schools with the Largest Libraries

You'll be hitting the books big time in law school. Not will you need a great repository of knowledge in which to do your research, but you'll be in competition for many of the same books with your fellow students. Worse, you'll be vying with a lot of other very determined people for a comfy seat, with a little privacy, near a window. So it makes sense that the larger the library, the bigger the target area, the easier it will be to get your hands on the text you want and find a place to curl up with it. But be warned: Big doesn't always mean accessible or tailored to your needs. Some libraries are large but built on a collection of esoteric junk that the donor of the building insisted that the library house. State system universities always look good in the number-of-branches department, but remember that the libraries listed as branches are usually at other schools with an entire student body fighting over access to those books as well. The following list is of universities with the largest libraries. The first number reflects the quantity of books in millions of volumes; the figure in parentheses is the number of branches on campus or in the school's state-wide system.

		Millions of volumes	Branches
1.	Harvard University, Cambridge, MA	12.8 million	(91)
2.	Yale University, New Haven, CT	10.2	(21)
3.	University of California, Berkeley, CA	8	(20)
4.	University of Texas, Austin, TX	6.8	(19)
5.	University of California, Los Angeles, CA	6.6	(15)
6.	Stanford University, Stanford, CA	6.5	(18)
7.	Columbia University, New York, NY	6	(21)
8.	University of Chicago, Chicago, IL	5.7	(9)
9.	Indiana University, Bloomington, IN	5.6	(28)
10.	University of Wisconsin, Madison, WI	5.3	(40)
11.	University of Washington, Seattle, WA	5.3	(22)

12. University of Minnesota, Minneapolis, MN	5.0	(18)
13. Ohio State University, Columbus OH	4.9	(51)
14. Duke University, Durham, NC	4.4	(11)
15. University of North Carolina, Chapel Hill	4.3	(16)
16. University of Arizona, Tuscon, AZ	4.0	(6)
17. Northwestern University, Evanston, IL	3.7	(11)
18. New York University, New York, NY	3.6	(8)
19. University of Georgia, Athens, GA	3.3	(3)
20. University of Pittsburgh, Pittsburgh, PA	3.3	(27)
21. University of Florida, Gainesville, FL	3.1	(16)
22. Southern Methodist University, Dallas, TX	3.0	(8)
23. University of California, Davis, TX	2.8	(6)
24. University of Hawaii, Manoa, HI	2.8	(2)
25. University of Colorado, Boulder, CO	2.6	(7)
26. University of Nebraska, Lincoln, NE	2.3	(12)
27. Vanderbilt University, Nashville, TN	2.3	(8)
28. Emory University, Atlanta, GA	2.2	(7)
29. Florida State University, Tallahassee, FL	2.1	(7)
30. University of Notre Dame, Notre Dame, IN	2.1	(1)
31. Tulane University, New Orleans, LA	2.1	(4)
32. Temple University, Philadelphia, PA	2.1	(12)
33. Boston University, Boston, MA	2.0	(24)
34. Georgetown University, Washington, DC	2.0	(4)
35. Case Western Reserve University, Cleveland, OH	1.9	(4)
36. Howard University University, Washington, DC	1.9	(9)

VIRTUAL VIRTUAL REALITY

Schools with the Most Computers On Campus

Virtually all schools have campus computer system link-ups that offer E-mail and online services to student dorms. Moreover, many schools offer computer-purchasing programs for those enrolled. But if you are not living on campus, you might need to use the school's computer center. All computer centers are not created equal, however, with widely varying numbers of computers available in the center. The difference is in the number of computers available in the center, since most have far fewer machines than students. On the other hand, the University of Minnesota's army of 20,000 computers serves a student body of 36,000—better than one computer for every two students. Regardless of a school's enrollment, the more machines a school has in its computer center, the better chance you have of finding one available when you need it. Here are the schools with the most computers for student access:

1.	University of Minnesota, Minneapolis, MN	20,000
2.	Stanford University, Stanford, CA	7,100
3.	University of Southern California, Los Angeles, CA	5,000
4.	University of North Dakota, Grand Forks, ND	3,500
5.	University of Illinois, Urbana-Champaign, IL	3,000
6.	Michigan State University, East Lansing, MI	2,500
7.	Temple University, Philadelphia, PA	2,000
8.	University of Connecticut, Storrs, CT	1,800
9.	University of Iowa, Iowa City, IO	1,600
10.	University of South Carolina, Columbia, SC	1,500
10.	University of South Dakota, Vermillion, SD	1,500
10.	University of Tennessee, Knoxville, TN	1,500
13.	Ohio State University, Columbus, OH	1,100
14.	Syracuse University, Syracuse, NY	1,000
14.	University of Chicago, Chicago, IL	1,000

14. University of Hawaii, Manoa, HI	1,000
17. University of Nebraska, Lincoln, NE	971
18. University of Virginia, Charlottesville, VA	950
18. George Mason University, Fairfax, VA	900
20. New York University, New York, NY	859
21. Rochester University, Rochester, NY	800
21. University of Georgia, Athens, GA	800
23. Florida State University, Tallahassee, FL	670
24. University of Florida, Gainesville, FL	612
25. Duke University, Durham, NC	600
26. University of Pennsylvania, Philadelphia, PA	555
27. George Washington University, Washington, DC	550

STATES WITH THE MOST LAW SCHOOLS

If for some reason, you and your law school do not have an immediate chemistry, it would be good to live in a state where there are more choices, a place where a person could start again after some minor mistake, an unavoidable altercation, or—God forbid!—a failure. For those of you who believe in second chances, here's a list of the states that have the most law schools.

1. California—19 law schools

California Western School of Law

Chapman University

Golden Gate University School of Law

Humphreys College

John F. Kennedy University

Loyola Marymount University

New College of California

Pepperdine University School of Law

Santa Clara University School of Law

Southwestern University School of Law

Stanford University School of Law

University of California—Berkeley, Davis, San Francisco, and Los Angeles

University of La Verne

University of the Pacific, McGeorge School of Law

University of San Diego School of Law

University of San Francisco School of Law

University of Southern California Law Center

University of West Los Angeles

Whittier Law School

2. New York—15 schools

Albany Law School of Union University

Brooklyn Law School

City University of New York, School of Law at Queens College

Columbia University School of Law

Cornell University Law School

Fordham University School of Law

Hofstra University School of Law

New York Law School

New York University School of Law

Pace University School of Law

St. John's University

State University of New York at Buffalo

Syracuse University College of Law

Touro College, Jacob D. Fuchsberg Law Center

Yeshiva University, Benjamin N. Cardozo School of Law

3. Illinois—9 schools

DePaul University College of Law

Illinois Institute of Technology, Chicago, Kent College of Law

John Marshall Law School

Loyola University of Chicago School of Law

Northern Illinois University College of Law

Northwestern University School of Law

Southern Illinois University School of Law at Carbondale

University of Chicago Law School

University of Illinois at Urbana-Champaign College of Law

3. Ohio—9 schools

Capital University Law School

Case Western Reserve University School of Law

Cleveland State University, Cleveland-Marshal College of Law

Ohio Northern University, Claude W. Pettit College of Law

Ohio State University College of Law

University of Akron School of Law

University of Cincinnati College of Law

University of Dayton School of Law

University of Toledo College of Law

3. Texas—9 schools

Baylor University School of Law

St. Mary's University School of Law

South Texas College of Law

Southern Methodist University School of Law

Texas Southern University, Thurgood Marshall School of Law
Texas Tech University School of Law
Texas Wesleyan University
University of Houston Law Center
University of Texas School of Law at Austin

6. Massachusetts—7 schools

Boston College Law School
Boston University School of Law
Harvard University Law School
New England School of Law
Northeastern University School of Law
Suffolk University School of Law
Western New England College School of Law

6. Pennsylvania—7 schools

Dickinson School of Law
Duquesne University School of Law
Temple University School of Law
University of Pennsylvania Law School
University of Pittsburgh School of Law
Villanova University School of Law
Widener University School of Law

8. Florida—6 schools

Florida State University College of Law
Nova Southeastern University

St. Thomas University

Stetson University College of Law

University of Florida College of Law

University of Miami School of Law

8. District of Columbia—6 schools

American University, Washington College of Law

Catholic University of America Columbus School of Law

District of Columbia School of Law

George Washington University Law School

Georgetown University Law Center

Howard University School of Law

8. Virginia—6 schools schools

William and Mary School of Law

George Mason University School of Law

Regent University School of Law

University of Richmond, The T. C. Williams School of Law

University of Virginia School of Law

Washington and Lee University School of Law

ONE-HORSE TOWNS

States with Only One Law School

There are certain places where you just can't afford to make a mistake. For instance, there are 13 states in the Union where they have only one law school. If you want to practice law in those states as an alumni of the one ABA-approved institution, it would be a good idea not to mess up once you get your foot in the door. There are two states—Alaska and Nevada—that have no law school at all.

Hawaii	University of Hawaii at Manoa, William S. Richardson School of Law
Idaho	University of Idaho College of Law
Maine	University of Southern Maine
Montana	University of Montana School of Law
New Hampshire	Franklin Pierce Law Center
New Mexico	University of New Mexico School of Law
North Dakota	University of North Dakota
Rhode Island	Roger Williams University School of Law
South Carolina	University of South Carolina School of Law
South Dakota	University of South Dakota School of Law
Vermont	Vermont Law School
West Virginia	West Virginia University College of Law
Wyoming	University of Wyoming College of Law

PART 2: LIFESTYLE

"Like prisoners in a dungeon too long, we want to get out but the prospect frightens us. We have grown accustomed to a static system in which no one, including us, has to take responsibility. Our memory of anyone making decisions is so distant that we equate giving responsibility with anarchy. We have been led to believe that government should operate like an error-free machine. Like the bureaucrats we despise, all we think about is what might go wrong, not what might get done.

"The cell doors are open wide to the verdant fields of free choice. But we pause when the wardens of modern law begin their matter-of-fact description of life outside their control. Law will no longer provide the final answer; bureaucrats will make decisions; people disagree; everything will depend. Uncertainty, they caution us, will descend upon society like the Dark Ages. We turn away from the opened door, and shuffle back to our places within the safety of the huge legal monument.

"The fears that keep us quivering in law's shadows are, in fact, the rudiments of a strong society. Constant exposure to uncertainty and disagreement is critical to everything we value, like responsibility, individualism, and community . . . .

"The effort to achieve social quiescence through clear rules, while plausible enough as a theory, has in fact infected the nation with a preoccupation with using law as a means to win: If the law is clear, we can fit ourselves into its words, and then—voilá—we get exactly what we want. But most services that a democratic society seeks to provide—decent education for all children, a practical and effective environmental law—are not win-or-lose propositions. Sensible results come out of discussion and negotiation, not from seizing technicalities and parsing legal language to achieve a victory . . . .

"Human nature turns out to be more complicated than the idea that people will get along if only the rules are clear enough. Uncertainty, the ultimate evil that modern law seeks to eradicate, generally fosters cooperation, not the opposite. Humans are driven to be reasonable with each other because uncertainty puts both at risk. The 'conflict' that modern law has preempted is what used to be known as give-and-take, the interaction that weaves the fabric of every strong community and healthy relationship."

—Philip K. Howard
The Death of Common Sense
Random House, 1994

LIFESTYLE 49

If you're really going to do your best in law school, you need the right atmosphere. Ambience is everything. How can you be expected to study if you're depressed because of the weather, or because you feel out of place? How will you be able to pay attention in class if you're worrying about getting a date for the weekend, and the pool of eligible date fodder is not exactly overwhelming? Your studies will absorb so much of your time, you can't afford to be bothered by avoidable environmental annoyances like speeding tickets, air pollution, and intemperate extremes of temperature. Of course, one person's opportunities are merely a distraction for the next student. This chapter will help you fit your choice of school to your personal lifestyle, your likes and dislikes, and whether you prefer the boondocks or the big city—high life or low, gleaming or grimy.

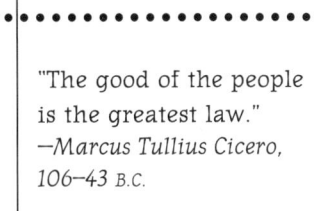

> "The good of the people is the greatest law."
> —Marcus Tullius Cicero, 106–43 B.C.

MOST ELIGIBLE MEN

Would school just not be the same without an abundance of male company? In each medical school on the following list, men outnumber women by at least two to one. The percentage of male students follows the name of the school.

1.	Thomas M. Cooley Law School	72%
2.	Regent University School of Law	69%
3.	Brigham Young University Law School	68%
4.	Baylor University School of Law	67%
5.	Mississippi College School of Law	65%
6.	Samford University, Cumberland School of Law	65%
7.	University of South Dakota School of Law	65%
8.	Franklin Pierce Law Center	64%
9.	Mercer University School of Law	64%

10.	Ohio Northern University, Claude W. Pettit College of Law	64%
11.	Gonzaga University School of Law	63%
12.	Texas Tech University School of Law	37%
13.	University of Arkansas School of Law, Fayetteville	37%
14.	University of Kentucky College of Law	37%
15.	University of Virginia School of Law	37%
16.	Vanderbilt University School of Law	37%

MOST ELIGIBLE WOMEN

In many medical schools, women are not even close to being equally represented. However, there is some hope. The playing field is much closer to even in some 40 institutions. That is to say, the ratio is nearly one to one. And in a very few schools, the percentage of women is a point or two higher than the male enrollment. The following is a list of medical schools where the percentages of men and women students is very close to 50/50.

1.	Northeastern University School of Law	60%
2.	Howard University School of Law	57%
2.	Loyola University, Chicago, School of Law	57%
4.	City University of New York School of Law	55%
5.	Stetson University College of Law	52%
5.	Suffolk University Law School	52%
5.	University of New Mexico School of Law	52%
8.	American University, Washington College of Law	51%
8.	North Carolina Central University School of Law	51%
8.	University of North Dakota	51%

FOR THE OLD FOGIES

Schools Where the Average Age of Students is 29 or Older

Law school is an arduous endeavor that will require deep thought and single-minded dedication. If you'd prefer not to be distracted by a young, hip, happening crowd, consider a school where the average age is almost 30. That's downright ancient. Most of them probably have twisted gray hairs growing out of their ears. Hey, that's not serious concentration—they're all asleep!

32

District of Columbia School of Law

30

City University of New York School of Law at Queens College

Texas Wesleyan University School of Law

29

Georgia State University College of Law

Seattle University School of Law

South Texas College of Law

Touro College, Jacob D. Fuchsberg Law Center

University of Maine School of Law

University of Montana School of Law

William Mitchell College of Law

FOR THE YOUNG AND THE RESTLESS

If you prefer a student body that's still growing and developing, or that looks more like the boys and girls on *Baywatch* than the folks on *Law and Order*, then you should pick a law school with the youngest students you can find. Young doesn't necessarily rule out fat and ugly, but it does improve the odds that no will have liver spots on their hands. Here are the law schools where the average age is the youngest.

Emory University School of Law	22
Boston University School of Law	23
Duke University School of Law	23
University of Alabama School of Law	23
Yeshiva University, Benjamin N. Cardozo School of Law	23

CULTURAL DIVERSITY

Schools with a Minority Enrollment of At Least 40 Percent

Do you refuse to live in a monochromatic world? Is an ethnic mix of students of many cultures and colors important to your education? Then choose a school from the following list of schools, where minority students make up at least 40 percent of the enrollment.

1. Howard University School of Law — 85% of 444 students
2. Texas Southern University, Thurgood Marshall School of Law — 77% of 541 students
3. University of Hawaii, Manoa, William S. Richardson School of Law — 72% of 241 students
4. Southern University Law Center — 58% of 339 students
5. North Carolina Central University School of Law — 55% of 306 students
6. University of New Mexico School of Law — 45% of 335 students
7. University of Washington School of Law — 40% of 468 students

MOST EXOTIC STUDENT BODY

Schools with the Highest Percentage of International Students

Why not go to a law school with an international flair? The air will be filled with foreign accents: French, Italian, Korean. You can wear a beret and put on cosmopolitan airs. Studying torts has got to be better in another language. Here are the law schools with the highest percentage of international students.

1.	Thomas M. Cooley Law School	29% of 1,740 students
2.	Detroit College of Law at Michigan State University	13% of 723 students
3.	University of Tennessee College of Law	12% of 482 students
4.	Cornell University Law School	10% of 569 students
4.	University of Hawaii, Manoa, William S. Richardson School of Law	10% of 241 students
6.	New York Law School	8% of 1,374 students
6.	University of Houston Law Center	8% of 1,018 students
6.	University of Richmond, T. C. Williams School of Law	8% of 481 students
6.	Whittier College School of Law	8% of 650 students

SCHOOLS WITH WOMEN AS FACULTY

The glass ceiling to advancement is securely in place in many fields, but women are finally breaking the barrier in academics. Perhaps you feel that a school that has demonstrated its commitment to equality of the sexes is better suited to your well being and your future. The following schools are rated by the percentage of female faculty members (both full and part time). The first list shows the 19 schools with a high percentage of women on staff, and the second is a list of 12 schools with low percentages of female faculty members.

The Top 19

1.	City University of New York, School of Law at Queens College	63%
2.	University of Richmond T. C. Williams School of Law	47%
3.	District of Columbia School of Law	45%
4.	North Carolina Central University School of Law	40%
5.	University of Hawaii School of Law	39%
5.	University of North Dakota School of Law	39%
7.	Widener University School of Law	37%
8.	Brooklyn School of Law	36%
8.	California Western School of Law	36%
8.	DePaul University School of Law	36%
11.	St. Thomas University School of Law	35%
11.	Loyola Marymount Law School	35%
13.	New York Law School	34%
14.	Nova Southeastern University School of Law	33%
15.	University of South Dakota School of Law	32%
16.	Arizona State University College of Law	31%
16.	Florida State University School of Law	31%
16.	Quinnipiac College School of Law	31%
16.	University of Florida School of Law	31%

The Bottom 12

1.	Louisiana State University School of Law	7%
2.	Emory University	8%
3.	Campbell University Norman Adrian Wiggins School of Law	9%
4.	George Mason University School of Law	11%
4.	University of Cincinnati School of Law	11%
6.	Regent University School of Law	12%
7.	University of South Carolina School of Law	13%
8.	University of Southern California School of Law	15%
8.	University of Toledo School of Law	15%
10.	Brigham Young University School of Law	17%
10.	University of South Dakota School of Law	17%
10.	Yale University School of Law	17%

FOR THE OPEN-MINDED

Schools with Organizations Providing Support for Gay and Bisexual Lifestyles

It is a sad commentary on America today that we feel constrained to make such a fuss over who we are allowed to love. That it has become part of the collision between liberals and conservatives in politics is particularly silly. The most obvious case in point is Newt Gingrich (whose sister is gay) and his stand against homosexuality. The labels *liberal* and *conservative* have nothing to do with accepting individuals for what they are—human beings, but they often signal the difference between those citizens who are open-minded and those who have closed up shop. Here are some schools at which organizations provide support for gay, lesbian, and bisexual lifestyles.

Cornell University Gay and Lesbian Alumni

Harvard Gay and Lesbian Caucus

Stanford University Gay and Lesbian Alumni

University of Washington Gay Alumni Association

University of Wisconsin Gay, Lesbian, Bisexual Alumni Council

SCHOOLS FOR ARCH CONSERVATIVES

Does the "L" word make your blood run cold? If you love Newt and The National Rifle Association, or if you haven't missed one of Rush Limbaugh's programs since he started on talk radio, or if you'd rather be dead than red, you need to make some prudent choices about where you attend school. Institutions of higher learning are notorious for fomenting revolution and fostering ultraliberal agendas. The following list includes the nation's conservative jurisdictions, where bleeding hearts are few and far between.

Alabama

The South is solid Republican these days. In both the 1992 and 1996 elections, the Republican candidates beat Clinton by over 100,000 votes—a margin that would have been even wider if Ross Perot hadn't been in the race, muddling the right wingers. Perhaps even more telling was the rumor circulated in April 1997 that Bobbie James, the wife of Alabama governor Fob James, Jr., had portraits in the governor's mansion removed because her spiritual advisor told her they were "demonized." We're talking fundamentalist with a capital F.

Samford University, Cumberland School of Law

University of Alabama, Tuscaloosa

California

Although California is often portrayed as the home of aging, hippie liberals and a world-class collection of kooks and sex fiends, some bastions of conservatism are also located in this state, most notably Orange County in the Los Angeles basin and counties south and west of the Bay Area. These are Republicans who think Attila the Hun was a reformer.

Pepperdine University School of Law

University of California at Davis

Loyola Marymount University

Santa Clara University School of Law

University of the Pacific School of Law

Georgia

The Peach State is a mixed bag: There's liberal Atlanta and Savannah, and then there's the rest of the state. Here are some schools in red clay country.

Mercer University, Walter F. George School of Law

University of Georgia School of Law

Idaho

Although the general population is a bit embarrassed by their presence, Idaho has more than its fair share of survivalist groups and right wing militias—and their ordnance.

University of Idaho

Kansas

In Kansas, a Democrat is one of those really hard-to-find items they put on the list to stump players in scavenger hunts. O. J. Simpson could probably win on the Republican ticket, because the party machine is so well established and supported by the citizenry in this state.

University of Kansas

Washburn University

Mississippi

This is arguably the most conservative state in the nation. People stand up at public gatherings when they hear the strains of "Dixie" playing, and they regularly argue over whether it's proper to fly the Confederate flag.

Mississippi College

University of Mississippi

Nebraska

Nebraska is home to vast herds of Republican elephants. The few Democrats in the state just try to keep from getting crushed by the stampede at election time.

Creighton University School of Law

University of Nebraska College of Law

North Carolina

There are two types of Tarheels: The liberals attracted to bustling Charlotte and the cultural aberration of Chapel Hill, and the rest of the state. By small margins, the conservatives have won out in the past two national elections. But to be among them, you need to go to the smaller cities.

Campbell University, Norman Adrian Wiggins School of Law

Duke University School of Law

North Carolina Central University

University of North Carolina, Chapel Hill

Wake Forest University

North Dakota

They'll have a January heat wave in Fargo before they vote liberal here. This is a stark landscape, populated by folks with a very strict interpretation of right and wrong, left and right. They're a long way from both coasts and they like it that way.

University of North Dakota

Oklahoma

There's a reason all those country and western songs about God, country, and the flag mention Oklahoma. This is more than a pickup truck with a rifle rack, family values kind of place. Oklahoma is a state of mind.

Oklahoma City University

University of Oklahoma

University of Tulsa

South Carolina

The Civil War started here at Fort Sumter, and many of the locals won't admit the war is over. They still speak of Strom Thurmond in hushed, respectful whispers.

University of South Carolina, Columbia

South Dakota

Ditto from North Dakota above—in fact they should probably merge into one big, conservative powerhouse of a state.

University of South Dakota

Texas

Texas is just too big to be easily categorized. The city folk make some elections close, but those cowboys and cowgirls in tumbleweed country keep the Lone Star state firmly in the Republican column. Here are the schools in areas where they have a bounty on liberals.

Baylor University School of Law

St. Mary's University School of Law

South Texas College of Law

Texas Tech University, School of Law

Texas Wesleyan University School of Law

Virginia

The left of center population of Virginia is clustered in the north, near Washington, most of the rest of the state remains deeply conservative.

Judge Advocate General's School

Regent University School of Law

University of Virginia School of Law

University of Richmond, T. C. Williams School of Law

Washington and Lee University

Utah

This is the promised land of the Mormons. They have a big cave in the side of a mountain in this state with genealogical records on every Mormon—and every American those Mormons are related to, going back generations. They helped Howard Hughes become the oddest billionaire in the world. Although the Mormon church no longer condones polygamy, there are several religious splinter groups who endorse multiple marriages for men. Not too long ago, it was next to impossible to buy an alcoholic beverage in this state. Mormons even eschew coffee, and they're not New Age by any stretch of the imagination. A conservative place to live.

Brigham Young University, J. Rueben Clark Law School

University of Utah School of Law

LOWEST UNEMPLOYMENT

If you will be seeking full or part-time work while attending law school, or if you intend on settling near your school, an area with a strong job market is important. Here are the metropolitan areas with the lowest unemployment rates, and the schools nearby.

San Francisco, California
3.3%. There's plenty of work in this beautiful city, but finding an apartment might be another matter.

Golden Gate University

San Francisco State University

Unversity of California, Hastings College of Law

University of San Francisco School of Law

Washington, DC, and its suburbs

3.4%. The United States government wants you.

American University, Washington College of Law

Catholic University of America, Columbus School Law

District of Columbia School of Law

George Washington University, The National Law Center

Georgetown University Law Center

Howard University School of Law

Seattle, Washington

3.5%. The joke used to be, "Last guy out of Seattle, turn out the lights." But with the aerospace industry back on track, the lights stay on.

Seattle University School of Law

University of Washington School of Law

Greensboro and Winston-Salem, North Carolina

3.7%. North Carolina has been booming since the Raleigh-Durham corridor became the Silicon Valley of the East, and since Charlotte became the center for regional business operations that have spread all up and down the East Coast.

Wake Forest University, Winston-Salem

Milwaukee, Wisconsin

3.8%. There must be something in the cheese. They're working in Wisconsin.

Marquette University School of Law

University of Wisconsin School of Law

Nassau and Suffolk, New York

3.8%. With the Atlantic Ocean in one direction and Long Island Sound to the north, it's suprising anyone works here at all.

City University of New York School of Law at Queens College

Brooklyn College of Law

Hofstra University School of Law

St. John's University School of Law

Touro College, Jacob D. Fuchsberg Law Center

Nashville, Tennessee
4.0%. Did Dolly Parton's Dollywood create *that* many new jobs?

Vanderbilt University

San Jose, California
4.0%. The heart of Silicon Valley is beating fairly well, but with technology stocks dropping, use caution.

Santa Clara University School of Law

Salt Lake City and Ogden, Utah
4.1%. A sure sign a city is growing—they got an NBA franchise in Salt Lake; but why did they call it the Jazz?

Brigham Young University, J. Rueben Clark School of Law

University of Utah School of Law

Cincinnati, Ohio
4.2%. After years of stagnation, the Midwest is making headway again.

University of Cincinnati School of Law

Oakland, California
4.2%. Who'da thunk it? Oakland is supposed to be tough and mean, but full of opportunity?

University of California, Berkeley

Portland, Oregon
4.2%. Portland has been the new Seattle ever since the latter became overpublicized and overrun.

Lewis and Clark College, Northwestern School of Law

University of Oregon School of Law

Willamette University School of Law

Minneapolis and St. Paul, Minnesota

4.3%. Together, these two cities are doing twice as well as the surrounding countryside.

University of Minnesota School of Law

Hamline University School of Law

William Mitchell College of Law

Columbus, Ohio

4.4%. Downtown Columbus has been rebuilt in the past several years, and the state capital has become a magnet for regional corporate headquarters.

Ohio State University College of Law

San Diego, California

4.5%. The Silicon Valley of the South, San Diego continues to grow into the wireless communications capital of America.

California Western School of Law

University of San Diego School of Law

Denver, Colorado

4.6%. If they can just keep that new airport open for a while, things might get even better here.

University of Denver School of Law

University of Colorado School of Law

Philadelphia, Pennsylvania

4.6%. If you have your heart set on the Northeast, this is one of the few urban areas that hasn't been clobbered by unemployment.

Temple University

University of Pennsylvania School of Law

Villanova School of Law

SCHOOLS IN THE STICKS

Does the frenzy of city life make you crazy? Do you like waking up to the scent of fresh air and a herd of cattle? Is walking that half mile out to your mail box, then hitting up Elsie for breakfast your idea of the perfect sendoff each morning? Then here is a list of law schools on the rural route (or at least within hiking distance of the boondocks). This is a great place to watch the tumbleweed blow by.

Campbell University, Norman Adrian Wiggins School of Law—This is a Southern Baptist institution, established in 1976 about 30 miles from the greater Raleigh, North Carolina, area in Bules Creek. This is probably where Opie grew up.

College of William and Mary School of Law—Williamsburg, Virginia, is where all the people make their living by dressing up like American colonists. Bring your knee britches.

Cornell University Law School—Ithaca, New York, is quiet, peaceful, serene, calm, mellow . . . did we mention quiet?

Pepperdine University—This school is located in Malibu. In fact, you can see the mighty Pacific from the campus and the evils of Los Angeles might as well be a thousand miles away, especially with the administration's emphasis on Christian ideals.

Ohio Northern University School of Law—The whole state of Ohio isn't exactly jumping out of its skin. Here's a hint about Ada, Ohio (the home of Ohio Northern): Its has a population of approximately 5,000 souls.

Stetson University School of Law—Deland, Florida, may be the most out-of-the-way hamlet in the Sunshine State, equidistant (read that as: "a good two-hour drive") from Orlando to the south and Daytona to the north. In Deland, there's no there there.

Southern Illinois University School of Law—We're talking plenty of room to spread out. The campus sprawls over 3,000 acres. When they say they're located in a rural area, they mean it—110 miles from St. Louis, in Carbondale.

University of Oklahoma College of Law—Norman, Oklahoma, as you might guess by its name, is a very small town 20 miles south of Oklahoma City. This is the kind of place where the intersection of First and Main Streets is a quiet location.

University of Vermont School of Law—On the White River in the Green Mountains, Royalton looks like it ought to be inside one of those glass snow globes you got for Christmas when you were a child.

University of Wyoming School of Law—There's nothing but wide open spaces from Laramie to the Grand Tetons. Get on your pony and ride.

West Virginia University College of Law—The nearest city to Morgantown, West Virginia, is in Pennsylvania. Pittsburgh is 77 miles away.

BIG CITY SCHOOLS

How're you gonna keep 'em down on the ranch once they see Dallas? If you like your air with a little texture and a few added minerals, or if you like living 20 or more stories above ground, then you might be a natural-born city slicker. This list is for those who want to be surrounded by a metropolitan area of a million inhabitants or more.

BOSTON, Massachusetts

Boston University School of Law

New England School of Law

Northeastern School of Law

Suffolk University Law School

NEW YORK, New York

Columbia University School of Law

Fordham University School of Law

New York Law School

New York University School of Law

Yeshiva University, Benjamin N. Cardozo School of Law

PHILADELPHIA, Pennsylvania

Temple University School of Law

University of Pennsylvania School of Law

Villanova University School of Law

PITTSBURGH, Pennsylvania

University of Pittsburgh School of Law

Duquesne University School of Law

DETROIT, Michigan

Detroit College of Law

University of Detroit, Mercy School of Law

Wayne State University Law School

ATLANTA, Georgia

Emory University School of Law

Georgia State University College of Law

WASHINGTON, DC

American University, Washington College of Law

Catholic University of America, Columbus School of Law

George Washington University Law School

Georgetown University Law Center

Howard University School of Law

MINNEAPOLIS/ST. PAUL, Minnesota

Hamline University School of Law

University of Minnesota Law School

William Mitchell College of Law

CHICAGO, Illinois

DePaul University School of Law

John Marshall School of Law

Loyola University School of Law

Northwestern University School of Law

University of Chicago School of Law

NEW ORLEANS, Louisiana

Loyola University School of Law

Tulane University Law School

HOUSTON, Texas

South Texas College of Law

Texas Southern University, Thurgood Marshall School of Law

University of Houston Law Center

DALLAS/FT. WORTH, Texas

Southern Methodist University School of Law

LOS ANGELES, California

Loyola Marymount University Law School

Southwestern University

University of California at Los Angeles School of Law

University of Southern California Law Center

Whittier College

SAN DIEGO, California

California Western School of Law

University of San Diego School of Law

SAN FRANCISCO, California

Golden Gate University School of Law

University of California, Hastings College of Law

University of San Francisco School of Law

SEATTLE, Washington

Seattle University School of Law

University of Washington School of Law

SUBURBIA, HERE I COME
Schools in the Suburbs

The majority of Americans grow up in a suburban environment. There's something comforting about a cul-de-sac. There are no big surprises, since everybody is just about the same—except for the two kids in high school who always wear black and probably sacrifice the neighbors' pets to Satan. Suburbia is not just a cultural blank, it's a state of mind. If you like living in the 'burbs and want to stay there, here are the schools for you.

Arizona State University School of Law—Tempe, AZ

Boston College Law School—Newton, MA

Northern Illinois University College of Law—DeKalb, IL

Northern Kentucky University School of Law—Highland Heights, KY

Nova Southeastern University, Shepard Broad Law Center—Fort Lauderdale, FL

Pepperdine University School of Law—Malibu, CA

Quinnipiac College School of Law—Hamden CT

Regent University School of Law—Virginia Beach, VA

Roger Williams School of Law—Bristol, RI

Samford University, Cumberland School of Law—Birmingham, AL

St. John's University School of Law—Jamaica, NY

St. Mary University School of Law—San Antonio, TX

St. Thomas School of Law—Miami, FL

Santa Clara University School of Law—Santa Clara, CA

Stanford University Law School—Stanford, CA

Touro College Jacob D, Fuchsberg Law Center—Huntington, NY

University of Michigan Law School—Ann Arbor, MI

University of Tulsa College of Law—Tulsa, OK

Western New England College School of Law—Springfield, MA

Widener University School of Law—Wilmington, DE

Whittier College of Law, Los Angeles, CA

CRIME RATES BY REGION

Though the rate of violent crime, burglary, larceny, and motor vehicle theft are all down dramatically in recent years (by 25 percent to 40 percent in most areas), some places are simply safer than others. Here is a list by region of the states with the higher crime rates in two catagories, violent crimes and crimes against property. The figures represent the number of reported crimes per 100,000 residents. States with large, metropolitan areas generally have higher crime rates. You should also remember that although university campuses are not immune to crime, they are still safe havens from most violent behavior, even in the worst of cities. Also, remember that the statewide crime rate may be quite different from the rate in the community in which the school is located.

	Violent Crimes	Crimes Against Property
New England		
Massachusetts	687.2	3,654.4
Connecticut	405.9	4,097.3

(Connecticut's murder rate of 4.6 per 100,000 residents is the worst in New England, thanks to the influx of youth gangs in the state's cities.)

Rhode Island	368	3,876.6
New Hampshire	114.5	2540.9

(New Hampshire is the safest place in New England.)

Middle Atlantic		
New York	841.9	3,718.3

(For all its bad reputation because of New York City, property crimes are relatively rare in New York state and are getting rarer.)

New Jersey	599.8	4,103.9
Pennsylvania	427.3	2,937.6
Midwest		
Illinois	996.1	4,459.6
Michigan	687.8	4,495.0
Indiana	524.7	4,106.8

Ohio	482.5	3,922.7
Wisconsin	281.1	3,604.0

(The least violent state in the area, by far.)

North Central

Missouri	663.8	4,456.8
Kansas	420.7	4,466.2
Nebraska	382.0	4,162.5

This state is mostly calm but has been impacted by youth gangs.

Minnesota	356.1	4,141.2
Iowa	354.4	3,747.5
South Dakota	207.5	2,853.1
North Dakota	86.7	2,779.6

This is the least violent state in the nation.

South

District of Columbia	2,661.4	9,512.1

(The nation's capitol is far and away the most violent and crime-ridden city in America. The murder rate is 65 per 100,000 residents. The next worst is in the teens.)

Florida	1,071.0	6,630.6
Louisiana	1,007.4	5,668.6

(Second highest murder rate: 17.2 per 100,000 residents.)

Maryland	986.9	5,307.9
South Carolina	981.9	5,081.0
Tennessee	771.5	4,591.2
Georgia	657.1	5,346.5
North Carolina	646.4	4,993.1

Alabama	632.4	4,215.7
Arkansas	553.2	4,137.7
Mississippi	502.8	4,011.7

(Third highest murder rate in the nation at 12.9 per 100,000 residents.)

Virginia, West Virginia, and Kentucky all have violent crime rates below the 500 per 100,000 mark. West Virginia's rate of violent crimes is down to 210.

West

Nevada	945.2	5,634.2
New Mexico	819.2	5,608.8
Arizona	713.5	7,500.1
Oklahoma	664.1	4,932.0
Texas	663.9	5,020.0
Colorado	440.2	4,956.1
Utah	328.8	5,762.0
Idaho	322.0	4,079.4
Wyoming	254.2	4.066.0
Montana	170.6	5,134.4

Pacific Coast

California	966.0	4,865.1
Alaska	770.9	4,982.9
Oregon	522.4	6,041.5
Washington	484.3	5,785.5
Hawaii	295.6	6,902.9

They don't hit each other much in paradise, but they sure do steal.

GOOD COPS, BAD COPS

The vast majority of police departments perform their job to the best of their abilities. They are, thankfully, the buffer between us and the predators. But in some places, due to overzealousness, corruption, or disorganization, sometimes the only way to tell the difference between the police and the criminals is to see who's wearing the badge. The following are lists of police departments with the best and worst reputations.

The Golden Doughnut Award: The Good Cops

New York City. For all the films about renegade cops, and the news stories about corruption in certain precincts, several things most be remembered about New York's Finest. First, there are perhaps 30,000 cops in the five boroughs, and relatively few are corrupt or violent. The vast majority are among the most professional and competent anywhere. The New York police don't bother you unless you're bothering someone or something else. They solve both large and small crimes as well as—or better than—most of their American colleagues. Like most New Yorkers, the cops have a brusque exterior, but they care, and it shows in their work. You're safer here than you might imagine.

Columbia University School of Law

Fordham University School of Law

New York Law School

New York University School of Law

Yeshiva University, Benjamin N. Cardozo School of Law

Dallas, Texas. Despite the lingering stigma after all these years of Kennedy and Oswald, and notwithstanding the harsh prisons and the state's eagerness to execute criminals, Dallas is symbolic of the efficiency of Texas police in general. The rate of violent crime in Texas is far below that of comparably populated states by a large margin. Some of the credit must go to the police. A doff of the Stetson to the Dallas cops.

Southern Methodist University School of Law

Montana. In a state this large, law enforcement is bound to have its shortcomings, but generally speaking, Montana has some of the best police officers in the country. This is one of the safest states in the nation. Some people attribute this to the fact that much of the citizenry walks around in Montana with a gun strapped to their hips. People in Arizona carry sidearms, too, but they tend to shoot one another in the southwest with alarming regularity. Montana is a remarkably non-violent place. The people respect the law and law enforcement officers. By all accounts, their respect towards the police is well founded.

University of Montana School of Law

San Francisco, California. This is probably the most liberal city in the nation, and the police department reflects that tolerance. Kept on a short leash, the SFPD is also a disciplined and talented force. San Francisco still has a bit of the Barbary Coast about it, and its reputation still attracts the young and footloose looking for a good time. The great thing about San Francisco is that you can have a lot of fun, and even go beyond the strict limits of legality in some cases, as long as you're not a nuisance or potentially harmful to yourself or others. The police in Babylon by the Bay won't let you get away with murder, but they're not going to bust you for jaywalking either.

Golden Gate University School of Law

University of California, Hastings College of Law

University of San Francisco School of Law

University of California, Berkeley

The Doughnut's Hole Award: The Bad Cops
Miami, Florida. Like California, Florida attracts criminals from across the country, so picking the decent tourists from the crooks isn't the easiest task. Unfortunately, the Miami Police Department's reaction to problems is too often overkill. They have long had a reputation for racial insensitivity, and a policy of shooting first and asking questions later.

University of Miami School of Law

St. Thomas University School of Law

New Orleans, Louisiana. With an annual rate of 17 murders per 100,000 residents, Louisiana enjoys the dubious distinction of being the most murder-prone state in the United States Most of the mayhem occurs in New Orleans, with the police contributing their fair share of violence. The New Orleans police department has had a number of its officers convicted of murder, including contract killings. Law enforcement is arrogant and inconsistent in The Big Easy.

Tulane University

Loyola University

Washington, DC. Students in DC should be required to wear body armor. There's a reason why the Washington Wizards, the city's NBA basketball team, was formerly known as the Bullets. Washingtonians bump each other off at the amazing annual rate of 65 per 100,000 residents, nearly four times the rate of runner-up, Louisiana. The police, it seems, show up only in time to toe tag the corpses. For many years, the capital recruited its police force among outsiders—country boys from West Virginia and other neighboring states, so the resulting police force had no vested interest in the community. While this situation has been alleviated to some degree in recent years, apparently the city could still use more and better police involvement.

American University, Washington College of Law

Catholic University of America, Columbus School of Law

George Washington University Law School

Georgetown University Law Center

Howard University School of Law

Oklahoma. "They don't care 'bout Dallas Texas/They don't care 'bout Wichita/If you're ever in Oklahoma/Better move easy 'round the law." So sang native Oklahoman J. J. Cale, who explained, "They'll take your money/they'll threaten your life/won't let you pass/without some strife." Sparsely populated Oklahoma has a higher crime rate than Texas, and notoriously tough cops. Say "Yes, sir. No, sir. Thank you, sir." Take your ticket and thank your lucky stars.

University of Oklahoma

Oklahoma City University

University of Tulsa

Los Angeles, California. There's trouble in paradise. While Joseph Wambaugh and TV shows dating back to the 1950s sang the praises of the "New Centurians," the actual Los Angeles police force behaved like the old Nazis for generations. The LAPD's reputation of being one of the most militaristic, racist, and violent departments in the nation is nothing new. The Rodney King incident and the offhanded disdain for individual rights shown by officers like Mark Fuhrman are a normal procedure for a police force allowed to run roughshod over simple civil rights. There is no good place to be a crime victim, but Los Angeles seems to be among the worst, considering the incredible bungling of airtight cases. There is something scary about a place where the *National Enquirer* solves a crime (Ennis Cosby's murder) before the local cops do.

Loyola Marymount University Law School

Southwestern University

University of California at Los Angeles School of Law

University of Southern California Law Center

Whittier College

MOST ANNUAL PRECIPITATION

Does anyone like rain besides farmers and the folks at the Totes umbrella factory? You can't get a tan if it's raining all the time. If you can't get a tan, you won't look your best. If you don't look your best, you won't feel good. If you're not feeling good, you won't be thinking good, and that could really mess up your plans for an LL.M. Most of the rain activity is concentrated in the Gulf Coast states, with a few exceptions scattered to the Northeast and Northwest. If you get depressed by light deprivation, and you hate wet feet, here are the schools to avoid.

Little Rock, Arkansas. It may have been more than ambition that drove President Clinton from Arkansas to Washington, DC. Little Rock experiences an average annual rainfall of 72 inches, the highest in the continental United States.

University of Arkansas, Little Rock

University of Arkansas, Fayetteville

Florida. The "Sunshine State" sees plenty of H_2O, from Miami's whopping 55.91 inches a year to Jacksonville, where the ground stays pretty darn damp with 51.32 inches of rain annually. But take heart: Most of the rain, especially in the warmer months, occurs in the afternoon—every afternoon, and in buckets full. The daily deluge usually lasts no more than half an hour, then it's back to fun in the sun.

Florida State University

Nova Southeastern University Sherd Broad Law Center

St. Thomas University

Stetson University

University of Florida

University of Miami

Mobile, Alabama. It rains in Mobile an average of more than an inch a week (63.96 inches annually), and it isn't much better upstate in Birmingham where they average 54.6 inches a year. That's why there's more Spanish moss than people in Alabama.

Samford University, Cumberland School of Law

University of Alabama School of Law

Georgia. The Okefenokee Swamp near Waycross, GA, is not an aberration. It's representative of much of the state. It's not a big surprise that a low-lying coastal town like Savannah gets almost 50 inches of rain a year. But Atlanta is a little worse at 50.77 inches.

Emory University

Georgia State University

Mercer University, Walter F. George School of Law

University of Georgia

New Orleans, Louisiana. A cool town, a fun town, a really wet town. If you've been there, you've noticed that they bury people above ground, because the water table is so high. New Orleans is almost underwater in any case, but it doesn't help that they get 61.88 inches of rain a year.

Tulane University

Loyola University

Galveston/Houston, Texas. They do things big in Texas. Galveston gets a saturating 42.28 inches of rain a year. But that's nothing compared to the weather they get in Houston: Tennis ball-sized hail and storms that could float Noah's Ark. It once rained out a baseball game at the Astrodome: The umpires couldn't get from their hotel to the stadium because of flooding.

South Texas College of Law

Texas Southern University, Thurgood Marshall School of Law

University of Houston

New York, New York. Many New Yorkers don't think of their city as having weather. But those who count the drops confirm that New York City drinks up a much-above-average 42.12 inches of annual rainfall. Albany and Buffalo upstate may brag because they get fewer inches a year, but most of theirs comes down as snow.

Brooklyn Law School

City University of New York School of Law at Queens College

Columbia University

Cornell University

Fordham University

Hofstra University

New York Law School

New York University

Pace University

St. John's University

Syracuse University

Touro College, Jacob D. Fuchsberg Law Center

Union University, Albany Law School

State University of New York Buffalo

Yeshiva Unersity, Benjamin N. Cardoza School of Law

Seattle/Tacoma, Washington. For all its bad reputation as the rain and drizzle capitol of the nation, the Seattle/Tacoma area experiences a relatively moderate 37.19 inches of rain annually. The real problem is, when it's not raining, it's cloudy. Sunshine is mostly a rumor in the Northwest.

Gonzaga University

University of Washington

Seattle University

Phoenix, AZ. No rain. At 7.66 inches of rain per year, they have the least precipitation of any major American city. If you see any spare rain around your neck of the woods, they'd appreciate your scooping it up in a pail and sending it to Phoenix today.

University of Arizona

Arizona State University

THE GOOD, THE NOT-SO-BAD, AND THE UGLY

Weatherwise, the following locations are the Good, the Not-So-Bad, and the Downright Ugly on the American landscape. The Good are places with the most temperate overall climates. The Not-So-Bad have a relatively moderate year with at least one horrendous season. The Ugly are places with flat-out crummy weather most of the year, excluding a few days here and there.

The Good

Honolulu, Hawaii. There is only one season in Hawaii—the gorgeous season. The January temperatures range between 66 and 80 degrees. July hovers between 74 and 88. The annual rainfull is only 22 inches, so this is paradise indeed.

University of Hawaii Manoa, William S. Richardson School of Law

San Diego, California. It is rarely too hot or too cold in Southern California. The average normal temperature in January ranges from 44 to 49 degrees, and in July the thermometer stays mostly between 66 and 76. With its scant 9.9 inches of annual rainfall, Southern California has one of the most temperate, sunny climates in the nation.

Los Angeles, California. Yes, there's the smog, but there's also a year-round mean temperature range of 49 to 84 degrees. Palm trees, oranges growing in your front yard—that's not too hard to take.

Loyola Marymount University Law School

Southwestern University

University of California at Los Angeles School of Law

University of Southern California Law Center

Whittier College

California Western School of Law

University of San Diego School of Law

Albuquerque, New Mexico. Most of New Mexico shares the dry, clear air of neighboring Arizona and Nevada, but Albuquerque's altitude eliminates much of the searing summer heat. The normal winter average temperature is a brisk 22 to 47 degrees, but in that dry mountain air (there are fewer than nine inches of annual rainfall here) it is the mildest 22 degrees you will ever experience. The summer range is a moderate 67 to 93 degrees.

University of New Mexico

The Not-So-Bad
Maine. There's no denying the frigid Maine winter. The January temperature range in Portland is between a rather nasty 11 degrees and 30 degrees and But for those who loathe hot weather, Maine is the place—they just don't have any. The temperatures in July range from 58 to 79 degrees. Anything over 80 is considered a heat wave.

University of Maine

Florida. Let's face it, the place is a steam bath in the summer. But ah, those South Florida winters that the retirees are so crazy for. For instance, the average winter temperatures in Miami range from 59 to 75 degrees. The Gulf Stream allows only a few freak freezes south of Orlando every five years or so. But don't trust those sunny brochures from schools in the northern half of the state—it gets almost as cold as Atlanta in Jacksonville, Gainesville, and Tallahassee.

University of Miami

Nova Southeastern University, Shepard Broad Law Center

St, Thomas University

Stetson University

Flagstaff, Arizona. Dry air notwithstanding, you'd have to be a lizard to wake up in the summer looking forward to 106 degrees outside. But January is a totally different story. The winter temperatures have been recorded in the teens in New Mexico, but you could live another hundred years and not see it happen. The normal winter temperature range is between 41 and 66 degrees.

Arizona State University

University of Arizona

Portland, Oregon. It's wet and dismal during the winter rainy season, with the mean temperature squatting between 34 and 45 degrees. But summers are dry and moderate, more like spring extended to September or October.

University of Oregon

Lewis and Clark College, Northwestern School of Law

Willamette University

The Ugly

The High Plains. Extending through parts of 13 states from the Dakotas down through the Texas panhandle south to Mexico, the High Plains were once called the Great American Desert. It starts were the rain ends in the East at about the 98th meridian. Forest gives way to grasslands and then to sage brush. The harsh weather anvil stretches all the way to the foothills of the Rocky Mountains and Denver. With long, hot summers and longer, freezing winters, this area makes up one fifth of the land mass of the continental United States. St. Louis, Missouri, is the gateway city to the Plains, and that anyone lives there is proof that Missourians are stubborn. The January temperature range is a wintry 21 to 38 degrees, and it's a rare summer that the mercury doesn't hit a hundred. Parts of Texas, Oklahoma, Kansas, Nebraska, North and South Dakota (they don't call it the badlands for nothing) are included in the High Plains and the generally intemperate weather.

University of Nebraska

Creighton University

University of Missouri, Columbia

St. Louis University

University of Missouri, Kansas City

University of Missouri, St. Louis

Washington University, St. Louis

University of North Dakota

University of South Dakota

University of Oklahoma

Oklahoma City University

University of Tulsa

Texas Tech University

University of Kansas

Washburn University

PART 3

ENTERTAINMENT VALUE

"Lawyers should be gagged, pure and simple. There'll always be leaks, but a judge with resolve can dream up sufficiently painful sanctions to make an attorney think twice before taking the risk. Next, kick cameras out of the courtroom. I didn't always feel this way. In fact, I started the Simpson trial believing that cameras could actually serve a useful purpose. Can you believe it—I thought they could actually teach the public what real trials were all about. The performance of the media in this case disabused me totally of that notion. The cameras in the Simpson courtroom not only encouraged lawyers to preen for the lens and prolong the life of every goddamn motion to increase their time on the air, it reduced a criminal trial to the status of a sporting event. *Court TV* has given rise to a bizarre burlesque of halftime commentary according to which one side or the other has 'won' or 'lost' on any given day. A criminal case is not won by the motion or by the day. Its outcome is determined by weeks and months of cumulative testimony. Until someone yanks the cameras, the public is continuing to be systematically miseducated about the process of justice."

—Marcia Clark with Teresa Carpenter
Without a Doubt
Viking, 1997

Attending law school is a very serious pursuit. Academics is in the forefront of everyone's mind who is struggling toward a LL. M. But let's face it, you can't think about torts, statute versus common law, obscure case studies, and moot court all the time. It would drive you nuts. All those mind numbing arguments, mumbo-jumbo wording of documents, and half-baked social contracts would send even the sanest person around the bend sooner or later. What good is the license to sue and thereby make beaucoup bucks going to do you when you're locked up in a loony bin somewhere with the key thrown away?

If you're going to perform at your peak in law school, and if you're going to justify your investment in tuition and all your early years of education, then you've got to make sure you get a minimum weekly allowance of undiluted fun and diversion. Obviously, it is imperative that you choose a school that allows you to partake in essential personal fun, either by providing the fun or being located in the proximity of fun and diversion. This chapter highlights some major sources of real big fun and lists the schools within easy striking distance. Hopefully you'll find your favorite kinds of fun here, use the information to make the right school choice, and totally avoid ending up gibbering to yourself and drooling all over your sweat-stained hospital gown. Take just a few minutes today to protect yourself and your future by making sure you can collect your fair share of fun in an organized and regular fashion.

> "The public regards lawyers with great distrust. They think lawyers are smarter than the average guy, but use their intelligence deviously. Well, they're wrong: Usually they're not smarter."
>
> –F. Lee Bailey
> Quoted in *The Los Angeles Times*, 1972

NEAR THE BEACH

When the going gets tough, do you just want to go to the beach? You're not alone. Sand and surf is a restorative for the soul, and the following areas provide some of the most perfect sand you'll ever get in your bathing suit. If you think the two most perfect words in the English language are "Surf's up!" pick your school from the following list.

Some of the most beautiful beaches in the country are found on the south shore of Long Island, **New York,** beginning at Long Beach and running East through Jones Beach, Robert Moses State Park, Fire Island, The Hamptons, Amagansett, and all the way to the lighthouse on Montauk Point. The swimming is great, and the people watching is even better—male and female bathing beauties of every nationality in the world throng to these beaches from the New York City metropolitan area. Under rarely experienced optimum conditions, the drive from Manhattan to Jones Beach State Park is a mere 45 minutes. Better to count on an hour-and-a-half commute each way.

On Long Island within 30 minutes of the beach:

St. John's University School of Law, Jamaica, NY

Hofstra University School of Law, Hempstead, NY

Touro College School, Jacob D. Fuchsberg Law Center, Huntington, NY

In the city within the 90 minute range of surf and sand:

Brooklyn Law School

City University of New York School of Law at Queens College

Pace University

Columbia University

Fordham University

New York University

New York Law School

Yeshiva University, Benjamin N. Cardoza School of Law

If you can handle the frigid temperatures of the North Atlantic surf, consider schools in the **Boston** area. Nearby the city are the beaches of Duxbury and Whitehorse. Within a few hours' drive are the graceful dunes and roaring waves of Cape Cod. Beyond the Cape, by ferry or small plane, are the island playgrounds of the rich and celebrated, Martha's Vineyard and Nantucket Island.

Boston College Law School, Newton

Boston University School of Law

Harvard University School of Law

New England School of Law

Northeastern University School of Law

Suffolk University School of Law

The **New Jersey** Shore stretches for over 100 miles from Atlantic Highlands to Cape May. The further south you go, the wider the sandy beaches become and the better the swimming and surfing. The choice locations are in the vicinity of Atlantic City—perhaps the birthplace of the American boardwalk. But if you like your salt air tinged with the smell of hot dogs and the hurdy-gurdy sound of the Ferris wheel wafting on the ocean breeze, visit the slightly weedy Asbury Park. You can make it to the beach in an hour, even from Philadelphia, via the Atlantic City Expressway.

Rutgers University School of Law, Camden, NJ

Rutgers University School of Law, Newark, NJ

Seton Hall University, South Orange, NJ

Temple University, Temple, PA

University of Pennsylvania, University Park, PA

Villanova University, Villanova, PA

You've got to really want to get to the beach to reach Ocean City, **Maryland,** and the Eastern Shore of **Virginia,** but these are some great summer retreats. The islands of Assateague and Chincoteague—once you get away from the motels—are filled with wildlife, seabirds, and miles of unoccupied sand. If you get tired of lying in the sun, you can take a day trip by ferry into the Chesapeake Bay to Smith Island or the more remote Tangier Island for the best blue crab in the world. These are the beaches that serve the **Baltimore-Washington, DC**, chunk of the East Coast megalopolis.

George Washington University, The National Law Center, Washington, DC

Catholic University of America, Columbus School of Law, Washington, DC

District of Columbia School of Law, Washington, DC

American University, Washington College of Law, Washington, DC

Georgetown University Law Center, Washington, DC

Howard University School of Law, Washington, DC

University of Baltimore School of Law, Baltimore, MD

University of Maryland School of Law, College Park, MD

George Mason University School of Law, Arlington, VA

Virginia Beach to the north and Myrtle Beach to the south flank the Outer Banks of **North Carolina** like two gaudy rhinestone clasps on the ends of a string of pearl-like beaches. The places in between are a national treasure: The wide dunes and pristine sands of these barrier islands are as unsullied as the neon-tinged, high-rise-pocked cities of Virginia Beach and Myrtle Beach are over-built and overrun. On the Outer Banks, you can roam the beaches where Blackbeard may have hidden his treasure. Just the names of places evoke the mystery of the sea and the adventure of sailing in the long-distant past: Cape Lookout, Cape Fear. One of the quaint island towns to spend time in is Okracoke, with its squat, white lighthouse. Plus it's a ferry port, in case you do get the urge to play Goofy Golf on a three-story miniature golf course with a bright turquoise waterfall tumbling over an imitation of the Pyramid of Giza.

College of William and Mary, Marshall-Wythe School of Law, Williamsburg, VA

Judge Advocate General's School, Charlottesville, VA

Regent University, Virginia Beach, VA

University of Richmond, The T.C. Williams School of Law, Richmond, VA

University of Virginia, Charlottesville, VA

University of South Carolina School of Law, Columbia, SC

Campbell University, Norman Adrian Wiggins School of Law, Bules, NC

Duke University, Durham, NC

North Carolina Central University, Durham, NC

University of North Carolina, Chapel Hill, NC

Wake Forest University School of Law, Winston-Salem, NC

Florida is one big sand bar sticking out into the water between the Atlantic Ocean and the Gulf of Mexico. Here you can experience every kind of beach atmosphere in one state—the tacky urbanism at South Beach in Miami; rugged and isolated surf along the northeast coast near St. Augustine, Jacksonville, and Fernandina; the retirees' dream of sugar-white sand and warm-as-weak-tea water in Clearwater, St. Pete, and in the panhandle at Pensacola. In Key West, you can stand where Hemingway may have stood looking at the confluence of the Ocean and the Gulf. Perhaps the only bad thing about going to school in Florida is that there's no better place to go for Spring Break.

Florida State University School of Law, Tallahassee

Nova Southeastern University, Shepard Broad Law Center, Fort Lauderdale

St. Thomas University School of Law, Miami

Stetson University School of Law, Deland

University of Florida School of Law, Gainesville

University of Miami School of Law, Miami

America's other ocean lover's paradise is **California**. Many of the state's 22 law schools are within a few hours' drive of the Pacific. While there is great, scenic splendor in the northern reaches—remarkable places like Big Sur and the rest of the Monterey Peninsula, Point Reyes, and Bodega Bay—the best beaches for frolicking in the waves without the protection of a wet suit are in Southern California, especially the San Diego area. The surf just gets better from there all the way down the Baja into Mexico. But if you prefer your beaches with an urban twist, there are Malibu, Venice Beach, and Santa Monica in L.A. and the place some people are calling neo-L.A., Santa Barbara.

California Western School of Law, San Diego

Golden Gate University School of Law, San Francisco

Loyola Marymount University School of Law, Los Angeles

Pepperdine University School of Law, Malibu

Santa Clara University School of Law, Santa Clara

Southwestern University School of Law, Los Angeles

Stanford University School of Law, Stanford

University of California Hastings College of Law, San Francisco

University of California School of Law, Los Angeles

University of San Diego School of Law, San Diego

University of Southern California School of Law, Los Angeles

Whittier College, Los Angeles

The last word in beaches is **Hawaii.** What more can be said, except apply early: The University of Hawaii at Manoa is taking only 140 students.

NEAR GREAT SKIING

The first skis, found preserved in bogs in Scandinavia and estimated to be 4,000 to 5,000 years old, were made from the large bones of extinct mammals. There's still something about mamboing down the fall line in deep powder that brings out the animal in human beings. Skiing is the closest thing to flying that a human being is capable of doing without leaving the ground. If you believe that a day spent on the slopes beats a day in classes any day of the week, then here are the schools for you:

Colorado. There's no competition. Colorado has more and better skiing than any other state in the Union. Just the names of the ski areas read like a snow mantra: Aspen, Snowmass, Vail, Keystone, Breckenridge, Copper Mountain, Steamboat Springs, Telluride, Monarch, Crested Butte, Glenwood, Durango, and Purgatory. And there are 20 more lesser known ski slopes sprinkled through the Rocky Mountains, which dominate the landscape. The snow is deep and powdery from at least mid-November until the late spring. If you like to strap sticks to your feet and slide down hills, come to Colorado.

University of Colorado School of Law, Boulder

University of Denver School of Law, Denver

Park City, Utah. Park City will be the site of the Winter Olympics in 2002. Get to school in the area immediately before the crowds of international rubberneckers beat the entire state into slush. Park City was probably the best undiscovered ski area in the nation until recent publicity about the worldwide competition descended on the village. The town is quaint, homey, graced with a gorgeous 19th century lodge, and the best—perhaps the only—sushi restaurant in Utah.

Brigham Young University, J. Rueben Clark Law School, Provo

University of Utah School of Law, Salt Lake City

Sun Valley, Idaho. The very first ski resort was developed in Sun Valley in 1936 by the Union Pacific Railroad. The owners installed the first successful chair lift on Dollar Mountain, and the rest is skiing history. Sun Valley is still a magical place to leave a few sitzmarks in the snow. The town itself, with a population of only 938, sits at an elevation of 6,000 feet, overlooking a pristine Alpine landscape locked in geological time—not much has changed in the 60-odd years since Sun Valley opened to the public.

University of Idaho School of Law, Moscow

Vermont. The Green Mountains form the granite backbone of this little state. With only 9,600 square miles in Vermont, there are still 24 alpine ski areas, including Killington, Stowe, Okemo, Stratton Mountain, West Dover, Warren, and Burlington. Perhaps no other state has been so untouched by the developers bulldozer blade and industrial pollution as Vermont. Despite temperatures that can dip well below zero, and the tendency of the local deep freeze to foster icy conditions on the slopes, Vermont consistently provides the best skiing in the East.

Vermont Law School, Royalton

NEAR GREAT ZOOS AND AQUARIUMS

Reconnecting with our neighbors on this planet is good for the spirit. Face to face with the animals displaced with our so-called civilization, you may find your world view forced into a different perspective. Not only is contact with the animal kingdom soothing for the soul, there is much to learn from the beasts. When you're feeling the stress of credit overload, there's no better way to relieve the tension than to bop down to the zoo and talk it over with Dumbo. Or test your future in business by making extended, syncopated eye contact with that marvelous killing machine, the great white, as he circles around and around at the aquarium. Here are the best places to talk to the animals in America, followed by the number of annual visitors at each and the nearby law schools.

	Annual Visitors
Sea World of Florida, Orlando	4,000,000
Stetson University, Deland	
Nova Southeastern University	
Shepard Broad Law Center, Fort Lauderdale	

University of Florida School of Law, Gainesville

Lincoln Park Zoological Gardens, Chicago, IL	4,000,000
John G. Shedd Aquarium, Chicago, IL	2,186,075
Chicago Zoological Park, Brookfield, IL	2,000,000

    DePaul University School of Law
    Illinois Institute of Technology Chicago, Kent College of Law
    Loyola University School of Law
    Northwestern University School of Law
    University of Chicago School of Law
    University of Illinois School of Law

San Diego Zoo, San Diego, CA	3,400,000
Sea World of California, San Diego, CA	3,000,000
San Diego Wild Animal Park, San Diego, CA	1,300,000

    California Western School of Law
    University of San Diego School of Law

National Zoological Park, Washington, DC	3,000,000

    American University Washington College of Law
    Catholic University of America Columbus School of Law
    District of Columbia School of Law
    Georgetown University Law Center
    George Washington University, The National Law Center
    Howard University School of Law

Busch Gardens, Tampa, FL	3,000,000

    Stetson University School of Law, Deland
    St. Thomas Univeristy School of Law, Miami
    University of Miami School of Law, Miami
    Nova Southeastern University Shepard Broad Law Center, Fort Lauderdale

St. Louis Zoological Park, St. Louis, MO	2,800,000

    St. Louis University School of Law
    Washington University School of Law

New York Zoological Park, Bronx, NY	2,000,000

    Fordham University School of Law, Bronx

Los Angeles Zoo, Los Angeles, CA	1,800,000

    University of California School of Law, Los Angeles
    University of Southern California School of Law
    Loyola Marymount University School of Law
    Southwestern University School of Law
    California State University, Los Angeles
    Whittier College School of Law

Monterey Bay Aquarium, Monterey, CA	1,700,000

    Stanford University, Stanford
    Santa Clara University, Santa Clara

National Aquarium, Baltimore, MD	1,500,000

    University of Baltimore School of Law
    University of Maryland School of Law

Marine World Africa USA, Vallejo, CA	1,454,000
San Francisco Zoological Gardens, San Francisco, CA	1,000,000

    Golden Gate University
    University of California, Boalt Hall, Berkeley
    University of California Hastings College of Law
    University of San Francisco School of Law

Milwaukee Zoological Gardens, WI	1,400,000

    Marquette University
    University of Wisconsin School of Law

Houston Zoological Gardens, Houston, TX	1,300,000

    South Texas College of Law
    Texas Southern University Thurgood Marshall School of Law
    University of Houston School of Law

Philadelphia Zoological Gardens, Philadelphia, PA	1,300,000

    University of Pennsylvania School of Law
    Temple University School of Law
    Villanova University School of Law

New England Aquarium, Boston, MA	1,300,000

    Harvard University School of Law
    Boston College School of Law
    Boston University School of Law

Suffolk University School of Law
New England School of Law
Northeastern University School of Law

Denver Zoological Gardens, Denver, CO — 1,300,000
    University of Denver School of Law

Cincinnati Zoo, Cincinnati, OH — 1,287,000
    University of Cincinnatti College of Law

Minnesota Zoological Gardens, Apple Valley, MN — 1,164,000
    Hamline University School of Law
    University of Minnesota School of Law
    William Mitchell College of Law

Sea World of Texas, San Antonio, TX — 1,000,000
    St. Mary's University School of Law

Metro Washington Park Zoo, Portland, OR — 1,000,000
    Lewis and Clark College Northwestern School of Law
    University of Oregon School of Law
    Willamette University School of Law

Sea World of Ohio, Aurora, OH — 1,000,000
    Case Western Reserve University School of Law, Cleveland
    Cleveland State University, Cleveland-Marshall College of Law
    Ohio Northern University Claude Pettit College of Law, Ada
    University of Akron School of Law
    University of Dayton School of Law
    University of Toledo College of Law

NEAR GREAT ROLLER COASTERS

There is no better practice for the ups and downs of life and business than to ride the nation's great roller coasters. The first version of this amusement park ride that would be recognizable as a roller coaster was the Russian Mountains, built in Paris in 1804 as a carriage running on an inclined track. It was an adaptation of timbered slides covered with ice—some as high as 70 feet—that had been built in Russia for public entertainment since at least 1650. A giant, wood-framed roller coaster became the legendary centerpiece of New York City's Coney Island, and similar rides soon spread to oceanfront boardwalks on both coasts. The last few years have seen a renaissance in the art of building roller coasters, with new materials and technology sending the industry into overdrive. Oddly enough, the American city with the most roller coasters per capita today is Las Vegas, as the gambling casinos branch out to grab the family vacation dollar. What a combination—craps, slots, poker, and roller coasters. If that's your pleasure, consider the University of Nevada in Lost Wages. And here are some other great local rides and the universities attached to them.

1. MONTU at Busch Gardens, Tampa, Florida. The world's tallest and longest inverted coaster is named after a hawk-headed, human-bodied Egyptian warrior god. The first vertical loop stands 104 feet tall and is followed by another six inversions. Track length is approximately 3,983 feet with a top speed of 60 miles per hour. Maximum drop is 128 feet. Ride duration, approximately three minutes.

   Stetson University School of Law, Deland
   St. Thomas University School of Law, Miami
   Nova Southeastern School Shepard Broad Law Center, Fort Lauderdale
   University of Miami School of Law, Miami
   University of Florida School of Law, Gainesville
   Florida State University School of Law, Tallahassee

2. LOCH NESS MONSTER at Busch Gardens, Williamsburg, Virginia. This steel, interlocking-loop coaster with two inversions is 130 feet tall. After an initial drop of 114.2 feet, the cars are going 60 mph for a running time of 2 minutes, 10 seconds.

   College of William and Mary, Marshal-Wythe School of Law
   Regent University School of Law, Virginia Beach
   University of Richmond, T. C. Williams School of Law

3. OUTER LIMITS: FLIGHT OF FEAR located at both Kings Island in Cincinnati, Ohio and Kings Dominion, Richmond, Virginia. The ride is experienced entirely in the dark. There is no chain lift. Escape velocity is attained via an electromagnetic wave that carries you from zero to 55 mph in 3.9 seconds. The track length is 2,705 feet.

University of Cincinnati School of Law, Cincinnati, OH
University of Richmond, T. C. Williams School of Law, Richmond, VA

4. WILD THING at Valleyfair, Shakoppe, Minnesota. Wild Thing is billed as one of the longest, tallest, and wildest rides in the world. It's 200 feet tall and more than a mile long. Cars will reach speeds up to 74 miles per hour. Hold onto your hat!

   Hamline University School of Law
   University of Minnesota School of Law
   William Mitchell College of Law

5. SUPERMAN THE ESCAPE at Six Flags Magic Mountain, Valencia, California. This is a state-of-the-art, gigantic L-shaped coaster. Vehicles blast out of the station, accelerating from 0 to 102 mph in seven seconds, and then shoot straight up the 41-story tower. The dual-track coaster spans more than 900 feet across the theme park, as much as 415 feet above the ground. The total track length is 1,235 feet.

   Santa Clara University School of Law, Santa Clara

NEAR GREAT MALLS

The first enclosed, climate-controlled mall was built in Edina, Minnesota in 1956, and by the early 1960s, malls began replacing Main Street in America. Today there are literally thousands of these concentrated shopping centers across the land, and a billion mall rats (teenagers who use the mall as a private hangout—maybe you were one). Malls also fostered the invention of the Valley Girl and have significantly added to the occurrence of shoplifting. Here are the megamalls for those of you who suffer withdrawal symptoms if you don't shop every day.

Atlanta, Georgia. The expression "shop till you drop" takes on an epic quality in Atlanta which boasts no fewer than 11 malls in the metro area. You can warm up at the Cumberland Mall with it's 145 stores on 72 acres; then try the Lenox Square on for size—212 stores on 63 acres of land. Better mark where you park here—the lot holds 7,000 cars.

Emory University School of Law

Georgia State University School of Law

Baltimore, Maryland. You can start at Eastpoint Mall (152 stores), then sink your teeth into Metro Plaza, where there are another 125 businesses.

University of Maryland School of Law

University of Baltimore School of Law

Bloomington, Minnesota. Here, just outside of the Twin Cities, resides the mother of all malls: The Mall of America. We're talking 500 stores! There are 66 restaurants, 29 woman's wear emporiums, 35 of what they call "unisex family clothing stores," and 13 different places that want to sell you jewelry. The only thing the place lacks on its 72 acres is a hotel—which you might need if you plan to traverse the entire place. But they're talking about expanding, so maybe that's next.

Hamline University

University of Minnesota School of Law

William Mitchell College of Law

Chicago, Illinois. Wear your walking shoes to Ford City. Its 142 stores are scattered over a whopping 100 acres.

DePaul University College of Law

Illinois Institute of Technology Chicago, Kent College of Law

The John Marshall Law School

Loyola University

Northwestern University School of Law

University of Chicago School of Law

Dallas, Texas. They do things big in Texas. Galleria Dallas packs 200 stores onto 43 acres. And if you can't find it here, there are seven other malls in town.

Southern Methodist University School of Law

Denver, Colorado. Working the Cherry Creek and Crossroads Malls could give you a Rocky Mountain shopping high, not to mention coronary arrest. Between them there are 320 stores on 102 acres.

Denver University

University of Denver

Jacksonville, Florida. Some people have entered the Avenues Mall and never been heard from again: 150 stores on 200 acres. Maybe they're looking for their cars in the 6,000 car lot. Or maybe they're over in Regency Square, where there are 170 more stores on 123 acres.

University of Florida School of Law, Gainesville

Miami, Florida. Mall-wise, Miami is the eye of the Florida shopping hurricane. There are 17 malls in the metro area. Three of them—Cutler Ridge, Dadeland, and Miami Intermall—have nearly 500 stores between them.

St. Thomas University School of Law

University of Miami School of Law

Houston, Texas. You think Dallas is something? Try The Galleria Houston version—310 stores. Oh, and there are another 15 malls in this city, too.

South Texas College of Law

Texas Southern University Thurgood Marshall School of Law

University of Houston School of Law

Los Angeles, California. Do they mall-shop in L.A.? Does a Valley girl talk through her nose? Try the Beverly Center, which crams 200 stores into eight acres. No luck? How about Century City, where there's another 140 stores. There are four other malls as well, but we're not going to tell you about them—you don't have enough money.

University of California School of Law, Los Angeles

University of Southern California School of Law

Loyola Marymount University School of Law

Southwestern University School of Law

California State University, Los Angeles

Whittier College School of Law

Missoula, Montana. Look long and hard at each and every one of the 130 stores in Southgate Mall. The next mall is a 170-mile drive.

University of Montana School of Law

Omaha, Nebraska. The locals take their prairie dollars over to Westroads Mall, where there are 200 stores on 60 acres.

University of Nebraska School of Law

Creighton University School of Law

San Diego, California. The city is fortified by nine malls. Foremost among them is Fashion Valley Center, laden with the temptations of 148 stores.

California Western School of Law

University of San Diego School of Law

San Francisco, California. If you can't find anything in your size in Embarcardo Centers' 150 stores, you can always drive five miles south to Stonetown Galleria, where there are 160 more wallet-emptying enterprises.

Golden Gate University School of Law

University of California Hastings College of Law

University of San Francisco School of Law

NEAR NATURAL WONDERS

The beauty of nature is an inspiration. The serenity and peace of the wilderness can sustain your flagging spirits and repair the frayed edges of your intellect and emotions. Everybody needs a tree to hug. Here are graduate schools for nature lovers.

Boston, Massachusetts. While there are no marquee natural attractions in Boston, there are three federally protected areas nearby: Great Meadows National Wildlife Reserve, Massosoit National Wildlife Reserve, and Parker River National Wildlife Reserve. Plus, there are no fewer than 31 separate state recreation areas in striking distance of the city.

Boston College School of Law

Boston University School of Law

Harvard University

New England School of Law

Northeastern University School of Law

Suffolk University School of Law

Bellingham, Washington. Sparsely populated, western Washington around the Bellingham area has incredible recreational potential. This is due to its glorious mountains and forests, including the federally protected Mt. Baker National Forest (452,000 acres) and the Northern Cascades National Park (281,000 acres). No one lives out here except Western Washington University students and maybe Bigfoot. By the way, if you run into the big fella, do us a favor—don't make it a Kodak moment. Sit him down, get him to talk on videotape, and if you can, make him sign an exclusive management contract.

Gonzaga University School of Law, Spokane

Seattle University School of Law, Seattle

University of Washington School of Law, Seattle

Boulder, Colorado. A big reason why Boulder became such a popular city over the past decade is its sheer natural beauty. Nestled in the foothills of the Rocky Mountains, Boulder is spectacular. There are two federally protected areas outside town: Rocky Mountain National Park (27,000 acres) and Roosevelt National Forest (136,000 acres).

University of Colorado School of Law, Boulder

University of Denver School of Law, Denver

Fresno, California. There is no city in the nation surrounded by more natural splendor. There are six federally protected areas, including Yosemite National Park, Sequoia National Forest, Sierra National Forest, Inyo Canyon National Park, Devils Postpile National Forest, and Kings Canyon National Park.

University of the Pacific, McGeorge School of Law, Sacramento

University of California School of Law, Davis

Honolulu, Hawaii. This island is surrounded by 135 miles of Pacific Ocean coastline and some of the finest weather on the planet. There's also the 1,900 acre Hawaiian Islands National Wildlife Reserve.

University of Hawaii, William S. Richardson School of Law, Manoa.

Laramie, Wyoming. In the northwest corner of the state reside two of the most magnificent of America's National Parks: Yellowstone and Grand Teton. There is nothing that quite compares with watching the Old Faithful geyser blow a stream of steam into the air every 50-odd minutes. The turquoise surface of Jenny Lake, at the foot of the Tetons, reflects a mirror image of the mountains' craggy peaks that is spectacular. Laramie isn't exactly around the corner, but you'll be closer than most everyone else.

University of Wyoming School of Law, Laramie.

Long Island, New York. The attraction here is salt water. The Fire Island National Seashore is truly something special—between hurricanes which tend to wash away the beach and a few hundred houses at a time, this narrow island is a haven for dune and sea life only a few short miles away from the East Coast megalopolis. There are also three National Wildlife Reserves on Long Island, and Jones Beach State Park—a world class ocean beach.

Hofstra University, Hempstead

St. John's University, Jamaica

Touro College Jacob D. Fuchsberg Law Center, Huntington

Miami, Florida. There are plenty of gangsters and little old ladies with blue hair, but there are also 84 miles of Atlantic Ocean coastline, plus the eerie, enormous Everglades National Park, not to mention the nearby fishing, snorkeling, and scuba diving offered by the Florida Keys.

St. Thomas University School of Law

University of Miami School of Law

Portland, Oregon. Besides the gigantic Mt. Hood National Forest (614,000 acres), the Siuslaw National Forest, 11 State Recreation Areas, a relatively short ride lands you in the venerable Redwood National Forest.

Lewis and Clark College Northwestern School of Law

University of Oregon School of Law

Willamette University School of Law

Rapid City, South Dakota. Besides the man-made monument to dead presidents, Mt. Rushmore, there's the starkly beautiful Badlands National Park and the Black Hills National Forest (395,000 acres).

University of South Dakota School of Law

Tucson, Arizona. The Grand Canyon is in the same state, and there are five other federally protected areas in proximity of Tucson, most notably Cabeza Prieta National Wildlife Reserve (416,000 acres) and the Organ Pipe Cactus National Monument (329,000 acres).

Arizona State University School of Law, Tempe

University of Arizona College of Law, Tuscon

Seattle-Bellevue, Washington. This area leads the country in suicides in large part because it rains here 160 days a year on average. The reason they all don't kill themselves is that there's great natural beauty to be seen through the mist: Mount Baker, Snoqualmie National Forests, and, 70 miles away, Olympic National Park.

Seattle University School of Law

University of Washington School of Law

NEAR GREAT MICROBREWERIES

If there is one essential nutrient all students need, it's beer. But not just any beer, and certainly not in a can—unless of course, nothing else is available or you've run out of cash and Bud Light is on sale for $4.59 a six-pack. No, the nation is being festooned with small beer breweries, marketing an incredible array of individualistic brews. If hops are your passion, and you care more about your beer's taste and character than its personality-altering effects when imbibed in mass quantities, the accessibility of microbreweries and their accompanying pubs should be factored into your search for the right school.

Boston and Cambridge. Schools include Boston University, Boston College, Suffolk University, Northeastern University, New England School of Law, and Harvard University.

1. Back Bay Brewing Co. (established 1995)
   755 Boylston Street, Boston
   (617) 424-8300
   This brewpub offers brews with a historical theme.
   Types of brew: 5 regulars, 1 seasonal
   Food style: funky World Cuisine

2. Boston Beer Works (established 1992)
   61 Brookline Avenue, Boston (across from Fenway Park)
   (617) 536-2337
   This is the largest brewpub (brewing volume) east of the Rockies.
   Types of brew: 12 regulars, 2 seasonal
   Food style: eclectic American

3. Brew Moon Restaurant & Microbrewery (established 1994)
   115 Stuart St. (Theatre District), Boston
   (617) 523-6467
   Brew Moon was voted Best of Boston/Best Brewpub by *Boston Magazine*; voted one of the Top New Restaurants by *Bon Appetit*, and awarded a Gold Medal at the 1996 Great American Beer Festival. It's located in the State Transportation Building and easily accessible by the T or by car.
   Types of brew: 5 regulars, 2–3 seasonal
   Food style: creative contemporary cuisine

4. Commonwealth Brewing Co. Ltd. (established 1986)
   138 Portland St. (West Side), Boston
   (617) 523-8383
   This well-established brewpub contains antiques from the Original Bass Brewery.
   Types of brew: 9 regulars, 1 seasonal
   Food style: American

5. Fort Hill Brew House (established 1996)
   125 Broad St. (Financial District), Boston
   (617) 695-9700
   Located in a renovated barn and factory.
   Types of brew: 6 regulars
   Food style: American

6. Brew Moon Restaurant & Microbrewery (established 1996)
   50 Church St. (Harvard Square), Cambridge
   (617) 523-6467
   This brewpub opened following the success of the Brew Moon in Boston. The pub has an "historically influenced interior design." which means everything looks old, but is really brand new.
   Types of brew: 5 regulars, 2–3 seasonal
   Food style: Creative contemporary cuisine

7. Cambridge Brewing Co. (established 1989)
   1 Kendall Square, Building 100 (Near MIT), Cambridge
   (617) 494-1994
   Types of brew: 4 regulars, 1–2 seasonal
   Food style: varies

8. John Harvard's Brew House (established 1992)
   33 Dunster Street (Harvard Square), Cambridge
   (617) 868-3585
   In this brewpub, you'll find what are purported to be William Shakespeare's Homebrew Recipes on display.
   Types of brew: 5 regulars, 1–3 seasonal
   Food style: American

New York. Schools include Columbia University, New York University, Fordham University, Brooklyn Law School, City University of New York School of Law at Queens College, New York Law School, Pace University, and Yeshiva University.

1. A. J. Gordon's Brewing Co. (established 1996)
   212 W. 79th Street (Upper West Side)
   (212) 579-9777
   Types of brew: 4 regulars, 1 seasonal
   Food style: varied, with great specials

2. Carnegie Hill Brewing (established 1995)
   1600 Third Avenue (Upper East Side)
   (212) 369-0808
   Offers Direct TV with sports on an eight-foot screen and 11 other TVs sprinkled all through the joint. Fireplace in the lower room.
   Types of brew: 3 regulars, 2 seasonal
   Food style: American

3. Chelsea Brewing Co. (established 1996)
   Pier 59, Chelsea Piers (West side)
   (212) 336-6440
   Near the fantastic Chelsea Sports Complex. Get lubricated and try climbing the 60-foot high rock climbing practice wall in the health club.
   Types of brew: 4 regulars, 2 seasonal
   Food style: American/Italian

4. Commonwealth Brewing Co. (established 1996)
   35 W. 48th Street (Midtown)
   Rockefeller Plaza
   (212) 977-2269
   This brewpub is an invasion of New York City by Boston's Commonwealth Brewery.
   Types of brew: 5 regulars, 1 seasonal
   Food style: Varied international

5. Hansen Times Square Brewery Restaurant (established 1996)
   160 West 42nd St. (Times Square)
   Broadway
   (212) 398-1234
   Offers authentic German-style brews in the inauthentic Disneyland atmosphere of the new Times Square. Not much character anymore, but the streets are clean.
   Types of brew: 3 regulars, 1 seasonal
   Food style: Varied

6. Heartland Brewery (established 1995)
   35 Union Square West (Greenwich Village)
   (212) 645-3400
   Located in historical Union Square District. It has hand-painted murals on the old, turn-of-the-century brick walls and canvas inlaid in its 40-foot back bar. Voted New York's best brewpub by *New York Magazine* and *New York Press*.
   Types of brew: 5 regulars, 3 seasonal
   Food style: American

7. Highlander Brewery (established 1996)
   190 Third Ave. (Gramercy Park)
   (212) 979-7268
   An American Bar & Grill with Scottish traditional flavor. Former site of Cheffield's German Beer Hall.
   Types of brew: 3 regulars

8. Typhoon Brewery (established 1996)
   22 East 54th St. (Midtown)
   (212) 754-9006
   Types of brew: 4 regulars
   Food style: Traditional Thai

9. West Side Brewing Co. (established 1993)
   340 Amsterdam Ave. (Upper West Side)
   (212) 721-2161
   Types of brew: 4 regulars
   Food style: American

10. Yorkville Brewery & Tavern (established 1994)
    1359 First Ave. (Upper East Side)
    (212) 517-2739
    Types of brew: 3 regulars, 2 seasonals
    Food style: American
11. Zip City Brewing Co. (established 1991)
    3 West 18th St. (Flatiron District)
    (212) 366-6333
    This brewpub was installed in the former home of National Temperance Society from the late 1800s. That's cheeky.
    Types of brew: 3 rotating varieties
    Food style: upscale pub fare

Chicago. Schools in this area include University of Chicago, DePaul University, Loyola University, Northwestern University, and, nearby, Northern Illinois University in DeKalb. This is an industrial city, so both these microbreweries are located in abandoned factories. It is an ambience of sorts.

1. Goose Island Brewing Co. (established 1988)
   1800 North Clybourn
   (312) 915-0071
   Types of brew: 2 regulars, 6 seasonal
   Food style: American
2. River West Brewing Company (established 1996)
   925 W. Chicago Ave.
   Types of brew: 8 regulars, 6 seasonal

Cleveland. Schools include Case Western Reserve University and Cleveland State University.

1. Great Lakes Brewing Co. (established 1988)
   2516 Market Street
   (216) 771-4404
   Located in an historic building in the Ohio City area.
   Types of brew: 3 regulars, 3 seasonals
   Food style: American Bistro

2. Rock Bottom Brewery (established 1995)
   2000 Sycamore St. (West Bank of the Flats, Downtown)
   (216) 623-1555
   Related through ownership to Denver's Rock Bottom Brewery.
   Types of brew: 7 regulars
   Food style: varied with Southwest flavor

3. Firehouse Brewery
   3216 Silsby Road, Cleveland Heights
   (216) 932-2739
   Brewpub located in landmark 1931 Tudor-style firehouse.
   Types of brew: 4 regulars, 2 seasonal
   Food style: varied from pub fare to fine dining

Washington, DC, and surrounding areas. Lots of schools. American University, Catholic University of America, District of Columbia Law School, Georgetown University, George Washington University, Howard University, and George Mason University.

1. Capitol City Brewing Co. (established 1992)
   1100 New York Avenue, Washington, DC
   (202) 628-2222
   Guided tours of brewery offered.
   Types of brew: 2 regulars, 7 seasonal
   Food style: American

1. Capitol City Brewing Co. (established 1992)
   2 Massachusetts Avenue NE, Washington, DC
   (202) 842-2337
   Located in an historic former postal building (sans Uzi-toting mail carriers) also offers an outdoor patio for alfresco dining and drinks.
   Types of brew: 6 regulars, 3 seasonals
   Food style: American

3. Virginia Brewing Co. (established 1995)
   607 King Street, Alexandria, VA
   (703) 684-5397
   Types of brew: 8 house
   Food style: Creole, seafood

4. Bardo Rodeo (established 1993)
   2000 Wilson Boulevard, Arlington, VA
   (703) 527-9399
   This is the largest brewpub in the country, sporting 24 pool tables. With that much fun inside, why the fake Southwestern getup? Just decoration is the best guess.
   Types of brew: 11 regulars, 2 seasonal
   Food style: Southwestern American

5. Blue 'n Gold Brewing Co.
   3100 Clarendon Blvd.
   Arlington, VA
   (703) 908-4995
   A highly recommended brewpub with New Orleans atmosphere.
   Types of brew: 6 regulars, 4 seasonals
   Food style: French creole

Austin, Texas. University of Texas, Austin

1. Bitter End Bistro & Brewery (established 1994)
   311 Colorado (Warehouse Arts District)
   (512) 478-2337
   Types of brew: 5 regulars, 1 seasonal
   Food style: Contemporary American

2. Copper Tank Brewing Co.
   504 Trinity St. (Sixth Street entertainment district)
   (512) 478-8444
   Types of brew: 5 regulars, 1–2 seasonal
   Food style: Various

3. Waterloo Brewing Co. (established 1994)
   401 Guadalupe Street (Sixth Street entertainment district)
   (512) 477-1836
   First brewpub in Austin, TX
   Types of brew: 5 regulars, 2 seasonal
   Food style: American grill

Seattle, Washington. Schools include Seattle University and University of Washington

1. Big Time Brewing Co. (established 1987)
   4133 University Way, N.E. (University District)
   (206) 545-4509
   This brewpub is only one block from University of Washington
   Types of brew: 3 regulars, 3 seasonal
   Food style: Pub fare

2. California & Alaska St. Brewpub (established 1991)
   4720 California Avenue
   (206) 938-2476
   This is the only brewpub to be found on Seattle's West Side.
   Types of brew: 8 regulars, 1 seasonal
   Food style: Pub fare

3. McMenamins Queen Anne (established 1995)
   200 Roy Street
   (206) 285-4722
   Just two blocks from Seattle Center and Key Arena.
   Types of brew: 7 regulars, 5 seasonal
   Food style: Various

Salt Lake City, Utah. University of Utah

1. Desert Edge Brewery at The Pub (established 1995)
   273 Trolley Square (Downtown)
   (801) 521-8917
   Only brewpub in area that brews traditional lagers.
   Types of brew: 5 regulars, 1 seasonal
   Food style: eclectic American

2. Fuggles Microbrewery (established 1994)
   367 West 200 South
   (801) 521-7446
   Types of brew: 12 regulars, 1 seasonal

3. Squatter's Pub Brewery (established 1988)
   147 West Broadway
   (801) 363-2739

Salt Lake City's first brewpub.
Types of brew: 10 regular, 2 seasonal
Food style: Both traditional and modern pub fare

SCHOOLS NEAR SOUR MASH BOURBON DISTILLERIES

Bourbon, that distinctly American drink, is distilled only in Tennessee and Kentucky. Jack Daniels is the benchmark by which all the other whiskies are measured. Unique in taste and mellow in its effects, J.D. is not simply a great drink: to many of its millions of devotees, it is the only drink. The distillery in Lynchburg, Tennessee, is now owned by Brown-Foreman, a conglomerate that produces about 20 various liquors, but the quality of Jack Daniels remains uncompromised.

The distillery tour is well worth taking. Step into the "aging shed," a wooden building about the size of two football fields with barrels stacked two stories high inside. Breathe in the essence of this noble liquor, let it permeate your pores, then walk back out into the sunshine—a religious experience. Jack Daniels recently introduced their first new whiskey in over a hundred years in an attempt to jump into the growing market for single barrel bourbons—Gentleman Jack. It is a superb sipping whiskey, even superior to Jack Daniel's Black (which is saying a lot). At about $25 a bottle, it's a bargain.

University of Memphis, Cecil C. Humphreys School of Law

University of Tennessee School of Law

Vanderbilt University, Nashville

The 200-year-old Jim Beam distillery claims a membership of 30,000 in its Jim Beam fan club, known as "The Kentucky Circle." That's nice—but of greater interest is its specialty sour mash whiskey priced at about $25 a fifth. Better yet is a group of what the company calls single-barrel whiskies priced in the $30–$50 range under names like Bakers, Brookers, Basil Hayden, and Knob Creek. All are excellent. Barton's Distillers of Clermont, Kentucky, also produce a fine single barrel along with their Kentucky Tavern and Ten High brands.

Bardstown, Kentucky is the home of Heaven Hill, a rather undistinguished bourbon. However, the company also produces Evan Williams, which is quite good and moderately priced.

Wild Turkey is distilled to its full 101-proof strength in Lawrenceville, Kentucky. Now the company is marketing a new variety, Rare Breed. Not a single-barrel bourbon, Rare Breed is a blend of different barrels of different ages to create a heavy but effective bourbon.

With everyone jumping on the bourbon bandwagon, it's no surprise that the Twelve Stone Company in Bardstown, Kentucky, is offering American Biker Bourbon. A portrait of a gentleman riding his hawg adorns the label. This picture—and the fact that the price is only about $13 a bottle—are all that recommends this drink. Don't offer it to any self-respecting biker—he or she might bust the bottle over your gourd. How could they presume to challenge the likes of Blanton's, distilled by the Sazerac Company in Frankfort, Kentucky? Sure, Blanton's single-barrel sells for three times as much as American Biker, but it's worth it.

Northern Kentucky University—Paul M. Helbert Law School

University of Kentucky School of Law

University of Louisville School of Law

IN WINE COUNTRY

If you count yourself a connoisseur of America's increasingly well-accepted home-grown wines and world class vintners, you might want to consider a school near the source of your favorite wine region. There are currently wine-producing vineyards in about 20 states. The following list includes the schools in the very best of Wine Country.

California

The Napa Valley

The Napa Valley, less than a two-hours' drive north from San Francisco, is about 3 or 4 miles wide in the south and extends north for 30 miles, narrowing down to less than a mile at the foot of Mt. St. Helena. More than 80 percent of Napa's workable land is under vine. But it is the quality, not the quantity, of the grapes that makes this region distinctive. In the 1960s, Napa began challenging European wine supremacy. Today, some of the best wines in the world come from this region. Here are the schools within striking distance.

Golden Gate University School of Law

University of California Hastings College of Law

University of California Boalt Hall, Berkeley

University of San Francisco School of Law

The Central Valley

About 90 percent of all the wine made in the America comes from California. Eighty percent of all California wines come from the Central Valley, stretching from Sacramento in the north to Bakersfield in the south. Here you will find the enormous Gallo Winery (with a 175 million gallon capacity, the largest in the world), and the University of California at Davis, the nation's leading wine school. The other schools in this large neighborhood include.

University of California School of Law, Davis

University of the Pacific McGeorge School of Law, Sacramento

Santa Clara University, Santa Clara

The Pacific Northwest

Oregon, Washington, and Idaho

Famous for light, "Northern European" style wines best grown in cool-climate vineyards, this area has carved itself a distinctive niche in the wine market. In Oregon, the best vineyards lie near the coastal regions around Portland. In Washington, the vintners have chosen Seattle and the Yakima Valley in the southeastern region of the state. The western regions of Idaho by the Snake River are also coming under successful cultivation.

Gonzaga University School of Law, Spokane, WA

Seattle University School of Law, Seattle, WA

University of Washington School of Law, Seattle, WA

University of Idaho School of Law, Moscow, ID

Lewis and Clark College Northwestern School of Law, Portland, OR

University of Oregon, Portland, OR

Willamette University School of Law, Salem, OR

New York State

Upstate and the Finger Lakes Region

New York makes more "bottle fermented" sparkling wine than California. New York's lambrusca grape wine country lies in the vicinity of Buffalo and to the southeast, in the center of the state. The scenic Finger Lakes region provides some great Cabernets, comfortable bed and breakfasts and The Bully Hill Winery—one of the finest in the state.

Cornell University School of Law

Syracuse University School of Law

Union University Albany School of Law

State University of New York School of Law, Buffalo

Long Island, New York

Long Island is developing an interesting wine growing district on its eastern extremity. The relatively temperate climate has begun to produce award-winning Sauvignon, Chardonnay and dry Cabernet wines. The wine-growing district is in the Bridgehampton and North Fork areas, about two hours away from New York City by car, if the Long Island Expressway doesn't happen to be transformed into a total parking lot the day you choose for an outing.

Brooklyn Law School

City University of new York School of Law at Queens College

Columbia University, New York City

Fordham University, New York City

Hofstra University, Hempstead

New York School of Law

New York University School of Law

Pace University School of Law

St. John's University School of Law

Touro College Jacob D. Fuchsberg Law Center

Yeshgiva University Benjamin N. Cardozo School of Law

Arkansas

The Altus Region

It ain't just moonshine coming out of the Ozarks anymore. Besides the north-central area of the state, the Altus Region at the Arkansas-Missouri-Oklahoma border was designated an officially controlled wine region in the mid 1980s. Actually, the area has been producing good wine ever since it was settled by Swiss immigrants in the 1870s. Here are the schools near what might become the next "sleeper" district of wine production.

University of Arkansas School of Law, Fayetteville

University of Arkansas School of Law, Little Rock

University of Tulsa School of Law, OK

NEAR GREAT TENNIS

1. **Queens, New York**. Huh? Well, Queens is the New York City borough that boasts the Forest Hills Tennis Stadium, home each August and September to the U.S. Open. If you can afford the tickets, you can munch $5 hot dogs while watching the greatest tennis players in the world compete.
Brooklyn Law School
City University of new York School of Law at Queens College
Columbia University
Fordham University
Hofstra University

New York School of Law
New York University School of Law
Pace University School of Law
St. John's University School of Law
Touro College Jacob D. Fuchsberg Law Center
Yeshiva University Benjamin N. Cardozo School of Law

2. **Boston.** The Longwood Country Club, in venerable Longwood, hosted the U.S. doubles championships between the 1920s and 1940s. It is still one of the premier tennis clubs in America today.
Boston College School of Law
Boston University School of Law
Harvard University, Cambridge
New England School of Law
Northeastern University School of Law
Suffolk University School of Law

3. **Newport, Rhode Island.** The beautiful Newport Casino, designed by Stanford White, is the Mecca of American tennis. The Casino houses the Tennis Hall of Fame and was the sight of the first U.S. Open Tennis championships in 1881.
Roger Williams University School of Law

4. **Sea Bright, New Jersey.** This lovely city on the Jersey Shore is the traditional American shrine for grass-court devotees. The old Eastern grass court circuit held their greatest amateur tournaments here and in the city of Orange between the 1920s and 1940s.
Seton Hall University, South Orange, NJ

5. **Los Angeles, California.** This city not only produced Ellsworth Vines and Ellis Marble, but it is also the place where the incomparable Bill Tilden spent his last years making tennis a celebrity sport through his friendships with Charlie Chaplin and many other Hollywood stars. L.A. remains the epicenter of West Coast tennis.
University of California School of Law, Los Angeles
University of Southern California School of Law
Loyola Marymount University School of Law
Southwestern University School of Law
California State University, Los Angeles
Whittier College School of Law

6. **Indianapolis, Indiana.** Thanks to its being the home of U.S. Tennis Association bigshot Stan Molless, Indianapolis hosts an important indoor tournament and offers tennis facilities and fervor equal to any tennis mad area in the country.
Indiana University School of Law, Indianapolis
Indiana University School of Law, Bloomington
University of Notre Dame, Notre Dame
Valparaiso University, Valparaiso

8. **Philadelphia, Pennsylvania**, and **Jacksonville, Florida**. American women's tennis was virtually born at Philadelphia's Belmont Cricket Club in the late 1880s. One of the most prestigious and pleasant tournaments on the Women's tour is the Bausch & Lomb Championship held each spring at the Amelia Island Plantation in Northeast Florida on the beach, not far from Jacksonville. Hear Monica Seles squeeze out her famous two-toned grunt with every backhand as she fights for her share of $450,000 in prize money.
University of Pennsylvania School of Law
Temple University School of Law
Villanova University School of Law
University of Florida, Gainesville

NEAR GREAT BASEBALL

1. **Tampa and St. Petersburg, Florida.** The majority of major league teams spend much of February and March each year around the Tampa–St. Pete area for spring training. Get a look at the coming season firsthand, long before it starts in earnest. You can't beat the weather either.
Stetson University School of Law, Deland
St. Thomas Univeristy School of Law, Miami
University of Miami School of Law, Miami
Nova Southeastern University Shepard Broad Law Center, Fort Lauderdale

2. **Savannah, Georgia**. This old seaport town happens to be home to the AA Savannah Cardinals. Sit close to the field at their cozy ballpark and catch the future stars before they start charging $50 apiece for their autographs.
Mercer University Walter F. George School of Law, Macon

3. **Phoenix, Arizona**. Like southern Florida, Phoenix is also a big spring-training camp for major league teams, only minus the ocean. But in the hot, dry air, you'll see plenty of 500-foot home runs.
Arizona State University School of Law, Tempe
University of Arizona School of Law, Tuscon

4. **Boston, Massachusetts.** Suffer along with Boston fans trying to overcome the "Babe Ruth Curse." For Red Sox rooters, baseball has transcended sport to become a religion. One of the truly great baseball towns.
Harvard University School of Law, Cambridge
Boston College School of Law
Boston University School of Law
Suffolk University School of Law
New England School of Law
Northeastern University School of Law

5. **Chicago, Illinois.** In the Windy City, you have the National League equivalent of the Red Sox: the Cubs. They're perennial bridesmaids and never the brides, but boy, do they have some fanatical fans. And if the Cubs aren't doing well . . . there's always the White Sox.
DePaul University School of Law
Illinois Institute of Technology, Chicago-Kent College of Law
The John Marshall Law School
Loyola University School of Law
Northwestern University School of Law
University of Chicago School of Law

6. **Cooperstown, New York**. Buried in the woods about 75 miles from Albany, easily accessible only by helicopter, is the Baseball Hall of Fame. Baseball was no more invented here than it was in Moscow. But the Hall of Fame is an incredible treasure trove of the game's history and artifacts. The baseball library is incomparable.
Cornell University, Ithaca
Syracuse University School of Law
Union University Albany Law School
University of Buffalo School of Law

7. **Philadelphia, Pennsylvania.** You will find the most critical baseball fans on Earth in the City of Brotherly Love. Here they not only booed Mike Schmidt, they'd boo anybody. These rabid but knowledgeable fans offer little love to those who can't play the game (and not much more to those who can).
University of Pennsylvania School of Law
Temple University
Villanova University School of Law

8. **New York, New York.** Come see Herr Steinbrenner's Yankees *and* the once-again dipsy-doodle Mets. Watch as players who starred with other teams around the nation crumble beneath the city's inexorable media microscope. And here's one for purists only: In the early 1840s, Alexander Cartwright initiated the first organized baseball team, the Knickerbockers, in New York City. The players—mostly firemen from different parts of town—practiced around the neighborhood now known as Murray Hill. In fact, take a pick and shovel up to the empty lot at 30th Street and Lexington Avenue and dig for baseball artifacts. Sell 'em and pay for your tuition.
Brooklyn Law School
City University of New York School of Law at Queens College
Columbia University
Fordham University
Hofstra University
New York School of Law
New York University School of Law
Pace University School of Law
St. John's University School of Law
Touro College Jacob D. Fuchsberg Law Center
Yeshiva University Benjamin N. Cardozo School of Law

9. **The Bay Area, California.** You risk frostbite at the Giants' windswept, foggy 3Com Park (still known as Candlestick Park, or The Stick, to those who love the place), or dying of loneliness watching the Athletics across the bay in Oakland. But at least you're in San Francisco.
Golden Gate University School of Law
University of California Hasting College of Law
University of San Francisco School of Law

University of California Boalt Hall, Berkeley
Stanford University School of Law

10. **Baltimore, Maryland.** Unlike the ugly, inhuman, and inhumane structures erected to house baseball in other cities, the Orioles' Camden Yards has integrity and charm. Unlike all the other owners, Baltimore's Peter Angelos refused to hire scabs during the last strike. This is a class-act franchise—and the crab cakes are good, too.
University of Baltimore School of Law
University of Maryland School of Law

11. **Denver, Colorado.** Join the baseball frenzy that has seen Colorado set astounding attendance records every year since the inception of their team. And when the Rockies aren't playing, there's the Rockies—the mountains that is. The beautiful foothills begin about 20 minutes away, outside Boulder.
University of Colorado, School of Law, Boulder
University of Denver School of Law

12. **Los Angeles, California.** Leave the game at Dodger Stadium in the seventh inning (like everyone else does) and drive over to Anaheim to watch the Angels. Nothing beats a two-team town.
University of California School of Law, Los Angeles
University of Southern California School of Law
Loyola Marymount University School of Law
Southwestern University School of Law
California State University, Los Angeles
Whittier College School of Law

13. **Buffalo, New York.** Buffalo? Yeah, Buffalo, home of the most successful minor-league franchise in the country. With the increasingly prima donna behavior of major leaguers, minor-league baseball has skyrocketed in popularity, and Buffalo is a bastion of the sport the way it ought to be.
State University of New York School of Law, Buffalo

14. **Arlington, Texas.** Think Texas is football country? Well, you're right—but they support their Rangers, and many of the experts have a sneaky feeling that this will be Texas's first championship baseball team.
Southern Methodist University School of Law, Dallas

NEAR GREAT HORSE RACING

1. **Louisville, Kentucky.** Not only is Louisville home to the first and brightest star in the triple crown, the Kentucky Derby, the state's bluegrass country raises many of the best thoroughbreds in the world.
University of Kentucky School of Law, Lexington
University of Louisville School of Law
Northern Kentucky University Salmon P. Chase College of Law

2. **Baltimore, Maryland.** Like Kentucky, Maryland is horse-friendly. Pimlico racetrack hosts the Preakness Stakes, second leg of the triple crown. And Maryland's horse farms are among the best.
University of Maryland School of Law
University of Baltimore School of Law

3. **New York, New York.** If you love to watch the ponies run in circles, there is no other place quite like New York. Besides hosting the third leg of the triple crown, the Belmont Stakes, at Belmont Park, the Big Apple offers adjacent Aqueduct Racetrack with a quality card for the entire winter. But be warned. If you're thinking of paying your tuition by betting against the locals, think again—New York horse bettors are among the meanest and savviest anywhere. There are few underlays (good, high-odds horses that haven't been discovered by every bettor at the track) here.
Brooklyn Law School
City University of New York School of Law at Queens College
Columbia University
Fordham University
Hofstra University
New York School of Law
New York University School of Law
Pace University School of Law
St. John's University School of Law
Touro College Jacob D. Fuchsberg Law Center
Yeshiva University Benjamin N. Cardozo School of Law

4. **Saratoga Springs, New York.** This quiet, historical town—site of a famous Revolutionary War battle—wakes up every August as the horsy contingent of high society flies into town from all over the world to participate in

Saratoga's summer meet and yearling auction. But it is also known as "the graveyard of favorites" because it rains here nearly every afternoon—no benefit to handicapping.
Cornell University, Ithaca
Syracuse University School of law
State University of New York School of Law, Buffalo
Union University Albany Law School

5. **Oceanside, New Jersey.** While there are plenty of city slickers attending the summer meet at Monmouth Park near the Jersey shore, you can still find underlays at Monmouth and at the relatively nearby Philadelphia Park.
Seton Hall University, South Orange
Rutgers University School of Law, Newark
Rutgers University School of Law, Camden

6. **Gulfstream and Hialeah, Florida.** Thanks to the influx of wiseguy New Yorkers, it's no bargain trying to outthink the locals during winter racing at these two south Florida tracks. But then again, it's January—and at least you're in Florida.
University of Miami School of Law
St. Thomas University School of Law
Nova Southeastern University Shepard Broad Law Center

7. **Santa Anita, California.** As the jewel of California tracks, you will see the best of West Coast racing here, but with the problems inherent in betting against a knowledgeable horse crowd. Angelino railbirds are as tough as they come.
University of California School of Law, Los Angeles
University of Southern California School of Law
Loyola Marymount University School of Law
Southwestern University School of Law
California State University, Los Angeles
Whittier College School of Law

7. **Delaware Park, Delaware.** This small track poses a double-barrel threat to your wallet. Should you tire of trying to beat the horses, you can retire to the banks of slot machines under the grandstand. Conversely, if you beat the slots, you can give it back at the betting windows. Take your pick.
Widener University School of Law

11. **Louisiana Downs, Louisiana.** Though adjacent to New Orleans and therefore prey to the city's resident sharks, and home of the prestigious Louisiana Derby, this track offers opportunities for the sophisticated bettor who can size up a horse and read between the lines of the racing form.
Loyola University School of Law
Tulane University

NEAR GREAT FOOTBALL

Green Bay, Wisconsin. This is the number-one pick for football fans, not because Green Bay won its first Super Bowl in 30 years in 1997, and not for the immortal Vince Lombardi and his teams of the 1960s, but because Packer fans eat, sleep, live, and die by their community-owned team, regardless of how it fares in the standings. Forget about Dallas and "America's Team." Look to the dairyland and "The People's Team."

University of Wisconsin School of Law, Madison

Marquette University School of Law, Milwaukee

Lincoln, Nebraska. Why would anyone want to settle here, adjacent to the High Plains notorious for having the coldest winters and hottest summers in the continental 48? The University of Nebraska Cornhuskers, for starters—the college football powerhouse of the '90s.

University of Nebraska School of Law

Creighton University School of Law

Canton, Ohio. This city gave birth to the legendary Canton Bulldogs, organized in 1905, when all players played both offense and defense—without helmets. Now Canton is the home of the Pro Football Hall of Fame.
Capital University School of Law, Columbus
Case Western Reserve University School of Law, Cleveland
Cleveland State University Cleveland-Marshall College of Law
Ohio Northern University Claude W. Pettit College of Law
Ohio State University College of Law, Columbus
University of Akron School of Law

University of Cincinnati School of Law
University of Dayton School of Law
University of Toledo School of Law

Jacksonville, Florida. The Bold New City of the South, they call themselves, but Jacksonville was on no one's map until the astounding Jaguars made it to the conference finals in just their second season of existence.

Florida State University, Tallahassee

University of Florida, Gainesville

Charlotte, North Carolina. Like the Jaguars, the Carolina Panthers amazed the football world by achieving a first-rate franchise in just their second year. The fans here have years of roaring for the great regional college football teams under their belts. This is not a football town for those with delicate systems.

Campbell University Norman Adrian Wiggins School of Law,
    Bules Creek

Duke University School of Law

North Carolina Central University School of Law, Durham

University of North Carolina School of Law, Chapel Hill

Wake Forest University, Winston-Salem

Dallas, Texas. Angering the rest of the country by arrogantly declaring themselves "America's Team," the Cowboys are now the prime example of American professional athletes run amok. Still, this is the most successful pro football franchise over the past 30 years, and you can bet they'll be back.

Southern Methodist University School of Law, Dallas

Notre Dame, Indiana. While the Fighting Irish have slipped in recent years, this most historically glorious of football schools now houses the College Football Hall of Fame.

University of Notre Dame School of Law

NEAR GREAT HOCKEY

1. **The New York metropolitan area.** There are three NHL teams within a slap shot of each other: the New Jersey Devils, the New York Rangers, and the New York Islanders. What's more, in the Rangers' Wayne Gretzky you can see the all-time leading scorer, the best playmaker in hockey history, and perhaps the greatest player ever to take to the ice.
Seton Hall University School of Law, Newark, NJ
Rutgers University School of Law, Newark, NJ
Brooklyn Law School
City University of New York School of Law at Queens College
Columbia University
Fordham University
Hofstra University
New York School of Law
New York University School of Law
Pace University School of Law
St. John's University School of Law
Touro College Jacob D. Fuchsberg Law Center
Yeshiva University Benjamin N. Cardozo School of Law

2. **Detroit, Michigan.** For many years, the Red Wings were led by the immortal Gordie Howe, widely considered to be one of the greatest players in the history of the game. Now, the Red Wings' leader is the brilliant Sergei Fedorov and his Russian teammates—the wave of the future in the NHL. In 1972, 94 percent of NHL players were Canadian. Today, the figure is 61 percent. Many of the non-Canadian players are American, but most of the best are European, specifically, Russian. Given the size of Russia and the lack of opportunity there, the trend is likely to continue. These Ivans can play.
Detroit College of Law at Michigan State University
University of Detroit, Mercy School of Law
Wayne State University School of Law

3. **Pittsburgh, PA.** The Penguins are blessed with the best one-two goal scoring punch in the NHL: the great Mario Lemieux (heir to Gretzky), and Jaromir Jagr.
Duquesne Univeristy School of Law
University of Pittsburgh School of Law

4. **Denver, Colorado.** The Avalanche is a new franchise that has reached the pinnacle of success in a fraction of the time that it previously took a championship team to build up steam. Colorado, a young, hard-checking team with plenty of depth, is likely to stay at the top.
University of Colorado School of Law, Boulder
University of Denver School of Law

5. **Miami, Florida.** The only other ice these people see besides the hockey rink is in their drinks, but The Florida Panthers are another young-but-poised squad that plays strong on the road as well as at home. A team of the future.
University of Miami School of Law
St. Thomas University School of Law
Nova Southeastern University Shepard Broad Law Center

6. **Philadelphia, Pennsylvania.** In years past, the Flyers were decried as a dirty-playing goon squad. They were also a darn good team. Now, led by Eric Lindros, they're ba-aaack. Just when you thought it was safe to go back on the ice.
University of Pennsylvania School of Law
Temple University School of Law
Villanova University School of Law

NEAR LEGALIZED GAMBLING

1. **Atlantic City, New Jersey.** The new Sodom and Gomorrah by the sea, it is considerably smaller than Las Vegas in terms of hotel rooms and total visitors, but out-grosses its Nevada counterpart in money wagered. With business going so well, perks and "comps" in Atlantic City casinos have diminished for the average visitor. These are reserved for the high rollers (read: proven suckers).
Rutgers University School of Law, Newark
Rutgers University School of Law, Camden
Seton Hall University School of Law, Newark

2. **Nevada.** Having legalized gambling in 1931, the casino business in Las Vegas and Reno is the most sophisticated in the nation, perhaps the world. Las Vegas is a city with slot machines in public restrooms. There are literally hundreds of places where you can gamble. Because of fierce competi-

tion, there are many perks, such as cheap or free food and lodging—if you can prove you're not a local. More importantly for the serious player, the house's take on slots and other rules can vary from casino to casino. Pay attention.
University of the Pacific, Sacramento, CA
University of California School of Law, Davis
Arizona State University School of Law, Tuscon, AZ
University of Utah School of Law, Salt Lake City, UT
University of Idaho School of Law, Moscow, ID

3. **Foxwood, Connecticut.** The American Indian has finally exacted his revenge on the white man in the form of the reservation casino. None is more successful than the Foxwood casino in west-central Connecticut. How successful? In July 1996, Foxwood had $849 million wagered in their slot machines alone. Rooms average $175 each. So bring your wampum.
Yale University School of Law
Quinnipiac College School of Law
University of Connecticut School of Law

4. **Iowa.** In 1989 Iowa approved river boat gambling along the Mississippi River in Sioux City and Dubuque. Moreover, their is slot machine gambling at three Iowa racetracks, Prairie Meadows, Bluff Run, and Dubuque.
Drake University School of Law, Des Moines
University of Iowa School of Law, Iowa City

5. **Illinois.** There are currently nine riverboat gambling casinos on the state's waterways. Areas excluded from the 1990 legalization were Lake Michigan and Cook County (Chicago). The principal locations for gambling are Joliet, Rock Island, and Alton.
Southern Illinois University School of Law, Carbondale
University of Illinois School of Law, Urbana-Champaign

6. **South Dakota.** In 1988, casino gambling in a limited form was legalized in Deadwood, South Dakota. Only poker, black jack, and slot machines could be played, with wagers limited to $5. To the dismay of the "plunger," but to the credit of the local voters, an attempt to raise the betting limit to $100 was defeated in a state referendum.
University of South Dakota School of Law

7. **Missouri.** Following the lead of neighboring Iowa, Missouri approved riverboat gambling in 1992. There are currently six floating casinos in St. Joseph and St. Charles.

St. Louis University School of Law
University of Missouri School of Law, Columbia
University of Missouri School of Law, Kansas City
Washington University School of Law, St. Louis

8. **Indiana.** The Hoosiers cut themselves a piece of the gambling pie in 1993, allowing riverboat gambling in several locations. It's a relatively small industry: There are only 243 gaming tables in the whole state.
Indiana University School of Law, Bloomington
Indiana University School of Law, Indianapolis
University of Notre Dame School of Law, Notre Dame
Valparaiso University School of Law, Valparaiso

9. **Kansas.** The staid folk of this Bible belt state-approved gambling on Kansas City river boats with restricted betting limits. There is also a casino on Indian land 17 miles north of Topeka.
University of Kansas School of Law, Lawrence
Washburn University School of Law, Topeka

10. **Minnesota.** The Mystic Lake Indian Casino operates on tribal land, attracting busloads of day tripping gamblers from as far away as Columbus, Ohio. There is absolutely nothing to distract you from the gaming tables on this reservation.
Hamline University School of Law, St. Paul
University of Minnesota School of Law, Minneapolis
William Mitchell College of Law, St. Paul

11. **Detroit, Michigan.** In January 1997, perennially impoverished Detroit decided to try and cash in on legalized gambling by approving "gaming with dice games." Neighboring Windsor, Ontario, had plenty of casino gambling, but the Canadian casinos do not have craps tables. These are banned in Canada because of an English law dating back to 1380, enacted by the King of England to keep his soldiers from blowing their paychecks on backgammon. Detroit is a winner.
University of Detroit Mercy School of Law
Detroit College of Law at Michigan State University
Wayne State University

12. **Mississippi.** Meandering further down the Big Muddy, we come to Mississippi, which allows riverboat casinos in two locations: in cities along

the Mississippi River and on the Gulf coast. There must be something in the water besides mud in the Mighty Mississippi to have inspired so many games of chance in so many otherwise conservative and straight-laced settings.
Mississippi College School of Law, Jackson
University of Mississippi School of Law, Oxford

13. **Louisiana.** In 1992, Louisiana followed the monkey-see, monkey-do tradition of state-sanctioned gambling by approving casinos a year after Mississippi did the same. Currently there are 11 casinos operating in New Orleans, Shreveport, and Baton Rouge.
Tulane University School of Law, New Orleans
Louisiana State University Paul M. Herbert Law Center, Baton Rouge
Loyola University School of Law, New Orleans
Southern University and A&M College School of Law, Baton Rouge

14. **Arizona.** In the vicinity of Tucson, there is the Desert Diamond Casino, operated by the Tohono O'odham Indians. This is the Old West scenery of John Wayne westerns, cheek by jowl with the lights and buzz of slots and the click of the poker chips.
University of Arizona School of Law, Tuscon

15. **California.** Sprinkled liberally across the state, there are 13,000 electronic slot machines operating on various Indian reservations, including the Crystal Mountain Casino outside of Sacramento on Indian land. The nearby state legislators are trying to close the place down. Stay tuned.
University of the Pacific School of Law, Sacramento

NEAR GREAT BASKETBALL

1. **Chicago.** Combine the incomparable Michael Jordan, the merely excellent Scottie Pippin, and the rebounding machine that is Dennis Rodman, and you have the Chicago Bulls, a team with depth in every direction. Jordan and Pippin are no longer young men, and Rodman is in constant danger of self-destruction. Sooner or later they will stop dominating the NBA. But don't hold your breath waiting.
Illinois Institute of Technology Chicago, Kent College of Law
The John Marshall School of Law
University of Chicago School of Law
Northwestern University School of Law
DePaul University School of Law
Loyola University School of Law, Chicago

2. **Miami.** Despite his Armani suits, slicked-back hair, avarice, and ego, Pat Riley can coach. Without using a single player drafted by the team, he has fashioned the Heat into a top-flight contender. Get out of the kitchen.
University of Miami School of Law
St. Thomas University School of Law

3. **Washington, DC** The Washington Bullets (interesting name for a team in the city with the highest murder rate in the nation) continue to misfire. But John Thompson's Georgetown Hoyas (alma mater of Patrick Ewing and Alonzo Mourning), remains a college powerhouse.
American University Washington College of Law
Catholic University of America Columbus School of Law
George Washington University, The National Law Center
Georgetown University Law Center
Howard University School of Law

4. **Los Angeles.** See the Hollywood stars ensconced in those TV camera-friendly court-side seats! See the 300 pound behemoth, Shaquille O'Neal, brutishly slam dunk his way to an astounding average 25 points per game! He may be a one-trick pony, this Shaq, but he may make the Lakers the next NBA dynasty.
Loyola Marymount University School of Law
Southwestern University School of Law
University of California School of Law, Los Angeles

University of Southern California School of Law
Whittier College School of Law

5. **Princeton, New Jersey.** Let's say you're a basketball nut with good grades—good enough to get you into an Ivy League school. Princeton is the place for you. As of this writing, the 1996–97 team is undefeated in its conference (11-0) and 10-3 against tougher, outside competition. This is nothing new at Princeton, which traditionally attracts smart guys who can play roundball.

6. **Boston.** Once proud, now clueless, the Celtics flounder in last place again. Still, there is basketball joy in Beantown thanks to Boston University and Boston College. Both Division I schools play right at the top of their tough conferences. And that includes the female side at Boston College, whose women's basketball team is one of the best in the Big East.
Boston College School of Law
University of Boston School of Law

7. **Seattle.** Thanks to superstars Shawn Kemp and Gary Payton, the Supersonics fly high over the Northwest. Both Kemp and Payton average 20+ points a game, with Kemp among the league leaders in rebounds and Payton likewise in assists. Both should be around long enough to lead Seattle past their usual playoff doldrums into the realm of truly elite NBA teams.
Gonzaga University School of Law, Spokane
Seattle University School of Law
University of Washington School of Law, Seattle

8. **Philadelphia.** Although the Philadelphia 76'ers are just about eighty-sixed off the NBA map, at least there is Villanova. In a town where the glass is always half empty, the Wildcats have earned raves with their fourth consecutive 20+ win season and by breaking the school record of 91 wins in four seasons.
Villanova University School of Law

9. **Connecticut.** By capturing the attention and admiration of the country, the women's basketball team at the University of Connecticut was a huge factor in the recent formation of a women's professional basketball league. It's difficult to say how the pro league will fare, but the Connecticut ladies keep rolling on.
University of Connecticut School of Law

NEAR GREAT GOLF

Admit it. The real reason you want a law degree is so you can spend three days a week on the golf course with the partnership's clients. If you are lucky enough to get a seat in the firm's golf cart one day, you'd better have a decent handicap. Pick your law school by its accessibility to great courses and golfing history.

1. The best on-campus golf courses of any U.S. colleges:
   University of Georgia
   Yale University

2. **Augusta, Georgia**. This small southern town, draped in Spanish moss and honeyed drawls, is the home of the most prestigious of Professional Golf Association Tournaments, The Masters, held annually at the Augusta National Golf Club.
   Emory University School of Law, Atlanta
   Georgia State University School of Law, Atlanta
   University of Georgia School of Law, Athens
   Mercer University Walter F. George School of Law

3. **Shinnecock Hills, Long Island.** It's one of the most venerable courses in the country, although you'll probably have to caddy to get on the course at all. Very snobby, very expensive.
   Hofstra University, Hempstead
   St. John's University, Jamaica
   Touro College Jacob D. Fuchsberg Law Center, Huntington

4. **Yonkers, New York**. Yonkers, just north of New York City, is *not* one of the world's garden spots. But it is where the St. Andrews Golf Course is located (named after the famous Scottish course where golf as we know it was devised). Founded in 1888, St. Andrews Country Club is the oldest American golf club.
   Brooklyn Law School
   City University of New York School of Law at Queens College
   Columbia University School of Law
   Fordham University School of Law
   New York School of Law
   New York University School of Law
   Pace University School of Law

St. John's University School of Law
Yeshiva University Benjamin N. Cardozo School of Law

5. **Newport, Rhode Island.** Golf was first taken up by American rich folk on summer vacation in Newport in the 1880s. The first U.S. Amateur Tournament took place at the Newport Golf Club in 1895. This is a great place to hang your knickers and spikes.
Roger Williams University School of Law

6. **Pebble Beach, California.** Located along the Monterey Peninsula, with some of the most breathtaking Pacific Ocean views on the West Coast as a backdrop, Pebble Beach Golf Club is perhaps the most beautiful and one of the most challenging courses in America today. And even though the course cost its new Japanese owners a lot of sushi, you can still play 18 holes here for only $150—not bad for a world-class course.
Santa Clara University School of Law, Santa Clara
Stanford University School of Law, Stanford

7. **Fort Worth, Texas.** Play the links of the Colonial Country Club and you are walking in the footsteps of perhaps the greatest of all golf legends—Ben Hogan. In fact, Hogan was instrumental in gathering the funding and the original membership for this fantastic course.
Southern Methodist University School of Law, Dallas

8. **Los Angeles, California.** Not only are there hundreds of golf courses in the L.A. area, this is also Tiger Woods's hometown. Woods is long and straight off the tee, and more accurate than other players on the PGA Tour who are consistently 50 yards shorter on their drives. And look at the prize money he's piled up in a year. Recommendation: Move to Los Angeles, follow Woods around, breathe the same air, see what happens—maybe his incredible talent will rub off. It could happen.
Loyola Marymount University School of Law
Southwestern University School of Law
University of California School of Law, Los Angeles
University of Southern California School of Law
Whittier College School of Law

9. **Bethpage, New York.** Of the thousands of public golf courses in America, the five in Bethpage, Long Island—The Red, Yellow, Blue, Green, and the 7,000 yard Black—are among the very best. How good is the Black? Good enough to host the U.S. Open in 2002.

Brooklyn College of Law
St. John's University School Law, Jamaica
Hofstra University School of Law, Hempstead
Touro College Jacob D. Fuchsberg Law Center, Huntington

NEAR GREAT STOCK-CAR RACING

There may be no sport in the United States so like the clash of gladiators as the competition on the NASCAR circuit. If, like many Americans, you have motor oil running in your veins instead of blood, then choose a school from the following list.

Daytona Beach, Florida. The headquarters of NASCAR and host to the crown jewel of the Winston Cup Series, the Daytona 500, launches each NASCAR race schedule and is also the site of the Pepsi 400 in mid-summer.

Florida State University School of Law, Tallahassee

University of Florida School of Law, Gainesville

Atlanta, Georgia. The Atlanta Speedway hosts the Primestar 500 around Easter and the final race in the Winston Cup series in the fall, the NAPA 500.

Emory University School of Law

Georgia State University School of Law

Darlington, South Carolina. The circuit moves to Darlington for the TranSouth Financial 400. (What kind of name is that for a stock-car race?) And the main event of the circuit on Labor Day is the Mountain Dew 500.

University of South Carolina School of Law

Fort Worth, Texas. The Texas Motor Speedway is home of the important Interstate Batteries 500.

Texas Christian University School of Law

Bristol, Tennessee. Bristol is the raceway used for the running of the venerable Food City 500 in the early spring. Then the first night race of the season is the Goody's 500 in August, with a starting time of 7:30 P.M.

University of Memphis, Cecil C. Humphreys School of Law

University of Tennessee School of Law, Knoxville

Vanderbilt University School of Law, Nashville

Talladega, Alabama. Talladega checks in with the Winston 500 in early April, then hosts the Sears Diehard 500 for the diehard men and machines as the schedule is winding down at the end of the circuit.

Samford University Cumberland School of Law, Birmingham

University of Alabama School of Law, Tuscaloosa

Sonoma and Fontana, California. They'll be saving tires and engines during Sonoma's short three-hour Save Mart 300, and Fontana is the site of the NAPA California 500 in late June.

University of the Pacific, McGeorge School of Law, Sacramento

University of California School of Law, Davis

Dover, Delaware. Dover's home to the Miller 500 on June 1, and the MBNA 400 in September.

Widener University

Pocono, Pennsylvania. The schedule starts heating up now as the stars, Jeff Gordon, Dale Jarret, Ricky Rudd, Sterling Marlin, Terry Labonte (last year's champ) and "Ironhead" Dale Earnhardt settle into the long groove of summer racing with The Pocono 500.

Temple University School of Law

University of Pennsylvania School of Law

Villanova University School of Law

Brooklyn, Michigan. This is the site of the Miller 400 in June and the ITW Devilbliss 400 in August.

Thomas M. Cooley Law School, Lansing

University of Michigan School of Law, Ann Arbor

Loudon, New Hampshire. Loudon replaces North Wilkesboro on the NASCAR circuit with the Jiffy Lube 300, and late in the season, the New Hampshire 300 at the New Hampshire International Raceway.

Franklin Pierce Law Center

Indianapolis, Indiana. Home of the famous Indianapolis 500 and one of the most important races on the NASCAR schedule, the Brickyard 400 in August.

Indiana University School of Law

Watkins Glen, New York. Watkins Glen is the site of the first Formula I Grand Prix of the United States, dating back to 1964. It remains an important Indy Car and stock car circuit track, playing host to many races, including The Bud in the Glen Race in mid-Summer.

State University of New York School of Law, Buffalo

Syracuse University School of Law

Union University Albany Law School

Richmond and Martinsville, Virginia. Richmond hosts the Pontiac Excitement 400 early in the season and the Miller 400 in September, one of two night races on the circuit. Martinsville is the headquarters for the Goody's 500 in the spring. If you show up in Martinsville wearing only your BVDs in late fall, they might make you eat your shorts at the gate of the Hanes 500.

University of Richmond, T.C. Williams School of Law

Regent University, Virginia Beach

University of Virginia School of Law, Charlottesville

Judge Advocate General's School, Charlottesville

George Mason University School of Law, Arlington

College of William and Mary, Marshall Wythe School of Law

Washington and Lee University School of Law, Lexington

Charlotte and Rockingham, North Carolina. Look to Charlotte for the grueling Coca-Cola 600 early in the season. The labor and management join hands in the UAW-GM Quality 500 in early October. Rockingham hosts the Goodwrench Service Race in the spring, and the AC-Delco in late October—the brands change, but the tension remains the same.

Campbell University, Norman Adrian Wiggins School of Law, Bules Creek

Duke University School of Law, Durham

North Carolina Central University School of Law, Durham

University of North Carolina School of Law, Chapel Hill

Wake Forest University School of Law, Winston-Salem

Phoenix, Arizona. A recent entrant on the circuit, Phoenix hosts the Dura-Lube 500 in the late Fall, the next-to-last race of the season.

Arizona State University School of Law, Tempe

University of Arizona School of Law, Tuscon

NEAR GREAT MUSEUMS

It takes many years of careful study to gain a true appreciation of great art. However, great art appreciates very quickly—it's a good investment if you know what you're doing. You won't be buying a Rubens or Rembrandt with your first Christmas bonus, but you should be knowledgeable enough about art not to snap up a bunch of fake Dali prints on the first excursion into the Art World. So visit a few museums, decide what you like, then snap up something with lasting value.

Atlanta, Georgia. Atlanta's High Museum of Art is a beacon of artistic heritage in the blank canvas of the Deep South.

Emory University School of Law

Georgia State University School of Law

Baltimore, Maryland. No weak sister to neighboring Washington when it comes to fine art, Baltimore offers eight museums including the noted Baltimore Museum of Art. And it's a short drive from there to the national collections in the country's capital.

University of Baltimore School of Law

University of Maryland School of Law

Boston, Massachusetts. These days we forget that Boston once was the cultural arbiter for the nation. The vestige of that power remains only in the phrase Banned in Boston. Boston contains no fewer than 25 museums, including the internationally renowned Museum of Fine Arts.

Harvard University School of Law, Cambridge

Boston College School of Law

Boston University School of Law

Suffolk University School of Law

New England School of Law

Northeastern University School of Law

Chicago, Illinois. The Second City in the United States (Los Angeles is still more a concept than a city) claims 19 museums, most notably the Art Institute of Chicago and the Museum of Contemporary Art.

DePaul University School of Law

Illinois Institute of Technology Chicago-Kent College of Law

The John Marshall Law School

Loyola University School of Law

Northwestern University School of Law

University of Chicago School of Law

Cleveland, Ohio. Cleveland? Yes, Cleveland. Local industrialists have thrown big bucks behind their civic pride over the years, and the residents have a right to be proud of the city's nine museums, particularly The Cleveland Museum of Art.

Case Western Reserve University School of Law

Cleveland State University Cleveland Marshall College of Law

Dallas, Texas. You've seen the soap opera reruns, now visit their museums (It won't take nearly as long as it took to find out who shot J.R.— there are only three museums dedicated to the arts in Dallas). If cattle and oil have you all tied up, then at least spend a day at The Dallas Museum of Art.

Southern Methodist University School of Law

Detroit, Michigan. Despite its recent woes as undertaker to the automotive industry in America, the city has long had a rich and diverse cultural life. Detroit offers eight museums. The Detroit Institute of the Arts and the Henry Ford Museum are outstanding.

Detroit College of Law at Michigan State University

University of Detroit, Mercy School of Law

Wayne State University School of Law

Fort Worth, Texas. Although smaller and living in the shadow of its neighbor, Dallas, Fort Worth has four museums, one more than Dallas. Of national prominence is the Fort Worth Museum of Art.

Texas Christian University School of Law

Los Angeles and Long Beach, California. Smog-besotted outside but culture-rich indoors, the Los Angeles basin is home to 33 museums, the greatest of which are the California State University at Long Beach Museum, the J. Paul Getty Museum (perhaps the best endowed cultural institution in the nation), and Los Angeles County Museum of Art.

University of California School of Law, Los Angeles

University of Southern California School of Law

Loyola Marymount University School of Law

Southwestern University School of Law

California State University, Los Angeles

Whittier College School of Law

Minneapolis–St. Paul, Minnesota. Two of the Twin Cities' six museums have achieved international renown. The Minneapolis Institute of Arts and the Minnesota Museum of Art.

University of Minnesota School of Law

New York, New York. For those of you who haven't been paying attention, New York is the planet's capital in many areas, including museums. Of the 52 museums in Gotham, at least seven are of world-class stature: American Craft Museum, Brooklyn Museum, Frick Collection, Metropolitan Museum of Art, Museum of Modern Art, Pierpont Morgan Library and Art Museum, and Solomon Guggenheim Museum.

Brooklyn Law School

City University of new York School of Law at Queens College

Columbia University

Fordham University

Hofstra University

New York School of Law

New York University School of Law

Pace University School of Law

St. John's University School of Law

Touro College Jacob D. Fuchsberg Law Center

Yeshiva University Benjamin N. Cardozo School of Law

Oakland, California. Go ahead and laugh, but Oakland has a respected cultural scene. There are two national standouts among the city's eleven musuems: Oakland Museum and University of California Art Museum.

University of California School of Law, Berkeley

Philadelphia, Pennsylvania. "All things considered," reads the tombstone of Philly native W.C. Fields, "I'd rather be in Philadelphia." The city takes a lot of guff these days on many fronts, but not so much from art lovers. There are 11 museums in this city, two of which are particularly respected: Pennsylvania Academy of Fine Arts and the Philadelphia Museum of Art.

Temple University School of Law

University of Pennsylvania School of Law

Villanova University School of Law

San Francisco, California. The 17 museums that grace the Golden Gate are eclectic in nature, like the city itself, including the Asian Art Museum of San Francisco, the Cartoon Art Museum, the Fine Arts Museum of San Francisco, and the Ansel Adams Center for Photography.

Godlen Gate University School of Law

University of California Hastings School of Law

University of San Francisco School of Law

Tampa–St. Petersburg, Florida. There are nine museums around Tampa Bay, but perhaps the most intriguing is the Salvador Dali Museum (Remember those prints we were talking about?). Don't miss the Scarfone Gallery

Stetson University, Deland

Washington, DC. The capital's museums rival those of Paris, Rome, London, and New York, and what's more, the vast majority of them have free admission. This is art for art's sake, and for the sake of the people. Of the 30 important museums here, at least 9 are as good as any on Earth: Corcoran Gallery of Art, Hirschorn Museum and Sculpture Gallery, National Gallery of Art, National Museum of African Art, National Museum of American Art, National Portrait Gallery, Phillips Collection, and The Wilderness Society's Ansel Adams Collection.

American University Washington College of Law

Catholic University of America Columbus School of Law

District of Columbia School of Law

George Washington University, The National Law Center

Georgetown University Law Center

Howard University School of Law

NEAR GREAT CLASSICAL MUSIC

Music soothes the savage beast and the savaged grad student. The following cities are standouts—among the top 25 cities in North America—in terms of musically related performing arts: ballet, opera, and classical orchestras. Quantity does not necessarily mean quality musical performance, so the cities have been listed alphabetically

Atlanta, Georgia. The cultural hub of the South has a ballet company, an opera company, and seven orchestras.

Emory University

Georgia State University

Baltimore, Maryland. Baltimore's ballet and opera companies each average 75 dates a year. Its orchestras present over 250 concerts annually.

University of Baltimore

University of Maryland

Boston, Massachusetts. One of the top 10 cultural centers in the United States, Boston has two ballet companies, four opera companies, and 23 orchestras.

Boston College

Boston University

Suffolk University

Northeastern University

New England College of Law

Harvard University, Cambridge

Chicago, Illinois. Chicago offers the musical cornucopia one would expect from a great American city, including a ballet company, nine opera companies, and 27 orchestras.

University of Chicago

De Paul University

Illinois Institute of Technology

Loyola University

Northwestern University

Detroit, Michigan. The metro area's orchestras perform at an average rate of better than one date a day. There are 12 of them here, and an opera company too.

Detroit College of Law at Michigan State University

University of Detroit Mercy

Wayne State University

Los Angeles, California. There are plenty of jokes about tinsel town. Los Angeles, though, is rated second in North America behind New York in terms of classical music by the Places Rated Almanac—a high lowbrow kind of burg. Three ballet companies, seven opera companies, and 25 orchestras call this place home.

University of California-Los Angeles

University of Southern California

Loyola Marymount University

Southwestern University

Whittier College

Milwaukee, Wisconsin. Milwaukee deserves mention for a fine, well-rounded musical agenda far out of proportion to its size. It has two ballet companies, three opera companies, and six orchestras.

University of Wisconsin

Marquette University

Minneapolis–St Paul, Minnesota. The nine orchestras in the Twin Cities play a combined total of nearly 500 dates a year. Three opera companies are also based here.

University of Minnesota

Newark, New Jersey. In the shadow of the megalithic New York scene, the Garden State centers its musical culture program in Newark with two ballet companies, four opera companies, and 12 orchestras.

Rutgers University

New York, New York. New York City is the classical music center of the nation—and of the world too. What are we talking about here? New York's 40 ballet companies, 35 opera companies, and 37 orchestras schedule over a thousand separate playing dates a year. What's more, five FM radio stations play over 500 hours of classical music a week.

Brooklyn Law School

City University of New York

New York Law School

New York University

Columbia University

Pace University

Fordham University

Yeshiva University

Philadelphia, Pennsylvania. Sixteen symphony orchestras, two ballet companies, and three opera companies are just the tip of the iceberg in this city.

University of Pennsylvania

Temple University

San Francisco, California. Definitely in the top ten American cities in terms of live musical performance, with three ballet companies, three opera companies, and nine orchestras. The classical tradition is yet a further jewel in the Gray Lady's crown.

Golden Gate University

University of California, Hastings College of Law

University of San Francisco

San Jose, California. Down the road from San Francisco, this burgeoning, silicon-powered city takes its culture seriously. Three opera companies and four orchestras reside here.

Stanford University

Santa Clara University

Seattle, Washington. The cultural mecca of the Northwest offers an escape from depression brought on by gray skies and constant drizzle, in the form of two ballet companies, two opera companies, and six orchestras.

University of Washington

Seattle University

St. Louis, Missouri. The local symphony is a world class outfit, playing in a world class hall. St. Louis is another city with a cultural life that far exceeds its size. A ballet company, an opera company, and six orchestras can be found here.

St. Louis University

Washington University

Washington, DC. The Wolftrap festival, the Washington Ballet, 21 orchestras, 9 operas, and a ballet company in the metropolitan area make the nation's capital a wonderful place to listen.

Catholic University of America

District of Columbia Law School

Georgetown University

George Washington University

American University

Howard University

NEAR ROCK AND ROLL LEGENDS

Duluth, Minnesota. Robert Zimmerman was born in this city in 1941 and grew up in Hibbing, a little mining town in the isolated northern reaches of the state. His father ran the local hardware store. In 1960, Robert left home to attend the University of Minnesota, but within a few months he had disappeared off the face of the earth and was reborn in New York's Greenwich Village as Bob Dylan, folk singer. Dylan has been a protest singer, a rock star, a born-again Christian, a saint to some, and a sellout to others. His songs, from "Blowin' in the Wind" to "All Along the Watchtower" to the more recent novelistic rock ballads like "Tweeter & the Monkeyman" (recorded with The Traveling Wilburys) constitute some of the most powerfully poetic lyrics in popular music. If you're a rebel and a poet, Minnesota's for you.

University of Minnesota School of Law

Hamline University School of Law
William Mitchell College of Law

Port Arthur, Texas. Lit by the gas flares of the cracking plants, Port Arthur is held together by rust, oil, and humidity. This industrial seaport, strapped onto the Sabine-Neches Ship Canal, became the birthplace of Janis Joplin on January 19, 1943. Looking around this town, there's no secret about where she got her grit. Janis ran away from home at the age of 17 to Houston and sang in country and western bands, moving on to San Francisco, where she hooked up with Big Brother and the Holding Company in 1966. One year later, she knocked 'em dead at the Monterey Pop Festival with her gut-wrenching rendition of "Ball and Chain." Success came fast and hard. By October 4, 1970, Janis had died of a drug overdose in Hollywood. See what you can do with these roots.

South Texas College of Law

Texas Southern University Thurgood Marshall School of Law

University of Houston School of Law

Freehold, New Jersey. If you feel a connection with blue collar guys, then maybe you would prefer New Jersey. Bruce Springsteen was born in Freehold on September 23, 1949. At the age of 13, he bought himself a guitar after seeing Elvis on television. By the early 1970s, he had formed the E Street Band and soon had a cult following of fans all over the Northeast. National stardom wasn't far behind. With the release of *Born to Run* in 1975 and his first national tour, Bruce truly became The Boss of American Rock and Roll. There is no better working-class love song than "Thunder Road." Don't get too wrapped up in rock and roll, though, or you'll end up a college dropout like Springsteen.

Seton Hall University School of Law, Newark

Rutgers University School of Law, Camden

Rutgers University School of Law, Newark

Memphis, Tennessee. There's only one place to go to school for a fan of Elvis Aron Presley, and that's near Graceland, a shrine to the memory of a man, his music, and his tasteless self-indulgence. Born in Tupelo, Mississippi, in 1935, The King started out as a pauper, the only son of poor sharecroppers who moved to Memphis in 1948. When Elvis was discovered in 1954 by Sam Phillips, the president of Sun Records, he had a high school diploma and was driving a truck. But his swiveling loins and shock of pomaded black hair soon had the sanitized world of American entertainment all shook up. "Heartbreak Hotel," "Hound Dog," "Don't Be Cruel"—his songs hit number one on the charts one after the other and stayed there. Maybe it was the Army, overwhelming fame, or Colonel Tom Parker that ruined the King, but except for a great televised Christmas special in 1968, Elvis ran too fat and out of steam after 1960. His last live performances in Las Vegas were trite and without passion. Elvis retreated behind the gates of Graceland with a band of fawning flunkies, and there he died of an accidental drug overdose in 1977.

University of Memphis Cecil C. Humphreys School of Law

Bay City, Michigan. She's a mother now, no longer a famous "virgin" in need of armpit grooming. Madonna Louise Ciccone was born here, near the shores of Lake Huron's Saginaw Bay in 1958. She has passed from the rock and roll scene into legend, a status bestowed on performers who find themselves getting a gazillion dollars for anything they choose to do (no matter *what* it is), and who have passed over from the "Hey, here I am! Take my picture, take my picture!" phase to the "Why won't they just leave me alone?" state of mind. You won't see Madonna's new baby here, but you might get some insight into "Who's That Girl" behind the bra.

Thomas M. Cooley School of Law, Lansing

University of Michigan School of Law, Ann Arbor

Augusta, Georgia. The Godfather of Soul burst on the scene in 1956 with his first successful single, "Please, Please, Please," and his influence on soul, rock, rap, and international music has reverberated far beyond his humble beginnings in Augusta, where he was born in 1933. His hits include, "Papa's Got a Brand New Bag," "It's a Man's World," and "Living in America." James Brown is out of jail again and is often spotted in northern Georgia, near his home. If you want to dig into the *real* roots of rap, talk to the Man. "Mama, come here quick, and bring me that lickin' stick!"

University of Georgia School of Law, Athens

NEAR GREAT COUNTRY AND WESTERN MUSIC

Nashville, Tennessee. The cradle of country music, and home of the Grand Ole Opry, Nashville is still the thriving, thrumming heartbeat of C&W, from the sequined, big band sound to retro cowboy songs. Stay out all night in the clubs lining the recently revitalized main drag downtown, listening to and dancing along with the best that Nashville has to offer. Tour the Opry and pretend you're the late great King of Country Music, Roy Acuff, whose reign on this stage lasted from 1938 to 1992. Visit the Country Music Hall of Fame, stand on Patsy Cline's sidewalk star, and maybe pick up some of the vibes left behind by the happiest girl in the whole U.S.A.

Vanderbilt University School of Law

Austin Texas. Stroll down Sixth Street in downtown Austin on a slow night, and you'll hear as much good music as anywhere in America. On the weekends, the town is simply gangbusters with great country and western acts. You could find yourself shaking hands with the late-blooming cult hero and "Zen cowboy," Jimmy Dale Gilmore. Get studio audience tickets for the recording of the PBS show "Austin City Limits" or share a beer with the Butthole Surfers, who call Austin home.

University of Texas School of Law, Austin

Bakersfield, California. Country and western music was stowed in the beat-up baggage of migrant farm workers, who moved to Southern California in their attempt to escape the Dust Bowl in the 1930s. The burg of Bakersfield became the Nashville of the West—without any of the Tennessee city's industry clout. But this is the place that roughed out the sounds of the likes of Buck Owens and the so-called C&W outlaws, Merle Haggard and Waylon Jennings (and, by extension, Dwight Yoakam). There are still plenty of pick-up trucks, dirt roads, and bars in and around Bakersfield if you want to stay in touch with your black-hat wearing outlaw side while working on your graduate degree.

University of California School of Law, Los Angeles

University of Southern California School of Law

Loyola Marymount University School of Law

Southwestern University School of Law

California State University, Los Angeles

Whittier College School of Law

ON THE LOLLAPALOOZA TOUR

Like a modern-day medieval market updated for cyberspace, the annual Lollapalooza Tour combines the best of alternative rock and world music with an astonishing advertising festival for every New Age practice and product in America. Get your belly button pierced again, donate all your extra change to rescue some obscure environmental cause, and then go bash your brains out in the biggest mosh pit in existence. And you don't have to pack up your puppy or jump in a day-glo painted van like the Deadheads. Here are the schools on the Lollapalooza Tour:

Seattle
University of Washington
Seattle University

Denver
University of Denver

Kansas City
University of Kansas, Lawrence
Washburn University, Topeka

St. Louis.
St. Louis University
Washington University

Indianapolis
Indiana University

Columbus
Capital University
Ohio State University

Chicago
Illinois Institute of Technology
The John Marshall Law School
Northwestern University
University of Chicago
Loyola University of Chicago
Depaul University

Detroit
Detroit College of Law at Michigan State University
University of Detroit, Mercy
Wayne State University

Boston
The New England College of Law

Harvard University, Cambridge
Boston College
Boston University
Northeastern University
Suffolk University

Philadelphia
University of Pennsylvania
Temple University
Villanova University

Pittsburgh
University of Pittsburgh
Duquesne University

New York City
Brooklyn College of Law
City University of New York
Fordham University
New York Law School
New York University
Columbia University
Pace University
Yeshiva University

Atlanta
Georgia State University
Emory University

Raleigh
University of North Carolina, Chapel Hill
Duke University, Durham
Campbell University, Bules Creek
North Carolina Central University
Wake Forest University, Winston-Salem

Austin
University of Texas, Austin

Dallas
Southern Methodist University

Phoenix
    Arizona State University, Tempe
    University of Arizona, Tuscon

Los Angeles
    University of California, Los Angeles
    Loyola Marymount University
    University of Southern California
    Whittier College

Sacramento
    The University of the Pacific, Sacramento

San Francisco
    University of California, Berkeley
    University of California Hastings College of Law
    University of San Francisco
    Golden Gate University

NEAR THE ALTERNATIVE ROCK SCENE

Louisville, Kentucky. Louisville is no longer just the city where you can stand with bowed head at Colonel Sanders's grave (in Cave Hill Cemetery) or have your name burned into a baseball bat at the Louisville Slugger factory. It is one of the hottest alternative rock generators in the nation featuring such groups as Rodan and Labradford.

University of Louisville School of Law

Raleigh-Durham–Chapel Hill, North Carolina. This is now the American capitol of alternative rock and roll ruled by Superchunk, the shark at the top of alternative music's food chain. The group has expanded their empire to include their own record label, Merge. Other happening groups rising from the new Silicon Valley of the East include Polvo and Porta-Static.

University of North Carolina School of Law, Chapel Hill

Duke University School of Law, Durham

Campbell University Norman Adrian Wiggins School of Law, Bules Creek

North Carolina Central University, Durham

Sake Forest University School of Law, Winston-Salem

Memphis, Tennessee. Memphis has recently seen the revitalization of the local music industry, with the Sun, Stacks, and Hi Labels all turning out new records by new rock groups. If you want to be in the know, go to school near Memphis and stand outside the Easley Recording Studios, where in the last year you could spot everybody from Aerosmith to Pavement to Sonic Youth.

University of Memphis Cecil C. Humphreys School of Law

Portland, Oregon. Yeah, Seattle was the birthplace of Jimi Hendrix and Kurt Cobain's Nirvana, but they're both dead now. You're more likely to see Alice in Chains and Soundgarden in the Astrodome than bumming around Puget Sound. The scene has moved on after all the overexposure, but it hasn't moved far. Try Portland, just east of Cape Disappointment. There are still plenty of old, bearded hippies staggering around and a fair share of yuppies moving in, but the alternative rock scene is vibrant and growing, fed by the local New Crafts movement and one of the biggest populations of goths in the country.

Lewis and Clark College Northwestern School of Law

University of Oregon School of Law

Williamette University School of Law

Lawrence, Kansas. This small town about 35 miles from Kansas City is known for chemical manufacturing, paper products, and pipe organs. The best known resident is the aging novelist supreme, William Burroughs, author of *Naked Lunch*. And last, but not least, Lawrence is recognized as the home of Flaming Lips, one of the hottest alternative rock groups to hit the American scene in years. They have emerged from a local music scene that is sure to be turning out plenty more antistar performers in the next few years. Get in on the ground level.

University of Kansas School of Law

MUST-SEE FILMS FOR LAWYERS

The following selection of classic movies are all related to the courtroom, lawyers, and the law. Don't miss them.

Twelve Angry Men —1957
Jurors struggle to determine whether a young Spanish American man is guilty or innocent of killing his father. The juror's prejudices and preconceptions about the trial, the defendant, and each other become magnified even though it appears to be an open and shut case. Based on a play written by Reginald Rose. Starring Henry Fonda as Mr. Davis (Juror #8). Also includes Joseph Sweeney as Mr. McCardle (Juror #9), Ed Begley (Juror #10), Jack Warden (Juror #7), Jack Klugman (Juror #5), E. G. Marshall (Juror #4), and Martin Balsam (Juror #1).

Witness for the Prosecution —1957
A rich, middle-aged widow is murdered and Leonard Vole is arrested. Sir Wilfrid Robarts agrees to defend him even though he recently suffered a near-fatal heart attack. To further complicate the defense, Vole's wife, his only alibi witness, agrees to be a witness not for the defense, but for the prosecution. Written by Harry Kurnitz, Larry Marcus, and Billy Wilder; based on a play by Agatha Christie. Starring Tyrone Power as Leonard Vole, Marlene Dietrich as Christine Vole, and Charles Laughton as Sir Wilfrid Robarts.

Anatomy of a Murder —1959
Laura Manion tells her husband she was raped. He kills the accused rapist, claiming crime of passion as his defense. Paul Biegler defends him, but must determine the motives of both the husband-murderer and the wife. Written by Wendell Mayes based on the novel by Robert Traver. James Stewart stars as Biegler, Lee Remick as Laura Manion, and Ben Gazzara as Lt. Manion.

Inherit the Wind —1960
Renowned lawyer Henry Drummond defends B. T. Cates, a teacher arrested for teaching Darwin's theories of evolution. Prosecutor Matthew Brady is a fundamentalist politician. Also referred to as the

1927 "Scopes Monkey Trial" on which it is loosely based. That trial featured the debates of Clarence Darrow and William Jennings Bryan. Based on the play written by Jerome Lawrence and Robert E. Lee, V. Starring Spencer Tracy as Drummond, Fredric March as Brady, and Dick York as Cates. Also includes Gene Kelly as E. K. Hornbeck, and Harry Morgan as the judge. The story was remade as a TV movie in 1988 written by John Gay, II, with Kirk Douglas as Brady, Jason Robards as Drummond (a role that won him an Emmy), Darren McGavin as Hornbeck, and John Harkins as the judge.

To Kill a Mockingbird —1962
This movie is told through the eyes of "Scout," a six-year-old tomboy. Tom Robinson is a young black man falsely accused of raping an ignorant white woman in a racially divided Alabama town in the 1930s. Atticus Finch is a lawyer who agrees to defend him. The townspeople want Atticus to pull out of the trial, but he refuses, of course. Written by Horton Foote; based on the 1960 Pulitzer Prize-winning novel by Harper Lee. Starring Gregory Peck as Finch, Mary Badham as Scout, and Brock Peters as Robinson.

The Verdict —1982
An ambulance-chasing, hard-drinking, down-on-his-luck lawyer, Frank Galvin, realizes that his medical malpractice case actually should go to court this time to punish the guilty and restore his dignity as a lawyer. Written by David Mamet; based on the novel by Barry Reed III, and starring Paul Newman as Galvin.

Legal Eagles —1986
District Attorney Tom Logan becomes involved with defense lawyer Laura Kelly and her client Chelsea Deardon, who is charged with the theft of a valuable painting. Logan is on the political path to a higher office until the women persuade him to investigate more deeply and to cut some official corners. Written by Jim Cash, Jack Epps Jr., and Ivan Reitman. Starring Robert Redford as Logan, Debra Winger as Kelly, and Daryl Hannah as Deardon.

The Accused —1988
Sarah Tobias is gang-raped by three men at her local bar. Kathryn Murphy, district attorney, tries to bring the men to justice and prove that there was no reason for Sarah to be attacked, even though she acted provocatively and had taken drugs. Written by Tom Topor and starring Jodie Foster as Tobias and Kelly McGillis as Murphy.

LAWYER JOKES

You're probably already getting tired of being the butt of all those lawyer jokes, and there are a million of them. But the only defense is to know the punch line and jump on it before the person harassing you can get the whole crowd at the bar guffawing at your expense. Finally there's a purpose for the Internet. A good lawyer has to keep current, so study these sites carerfully.

Websites with great lawyer jokes:

1. http://radbruch.jura.uni-mainz.de/jur_res_auf_rad/lawyer.html
   What's the difference between God and a lawyer? God doesn't think he's a lawyer.
2. http://www.bcl.net/~kbb/funny.html
   A lawyer died and arrived at the Pearly Gates. To his dismay, there were thousands of people ahead of him in line to see St. Peter. To his surprise, St. Peter left his desk at the gate and came down the long line to where the lawyer was and greeted him warmly. Then St. Peter and one of his assistants took the lawyer by the hands and guided him up to the front of the line and into a comfortable chair by his desk. The lawyer said, "I don't mind all this attention, but what makes me so special?" St. Peter replied, "Well, I've added up all the hours for which you billed your clients, and by my calculations you must be about 193 years old!"

"How can I ever thank you?" gushed a woman to Clarence Darrow, after he had solved her legal troubles. "My dear woman," Darrow replied, "ever since the Phoenicians invented money there has been only one answer to that question."

CHECK OUT THESE OTHER SITES:

3. http://www.emeraldis.com/~rrichardson/jokes.htm
4. http://www.aznvlaw.com/lawyerjokes.html
5. http://www.ironclad.com/lawyerjokes/courtroom.html
6. http://www.octonline.com/webpages/user/paheerathan/lawyer.htm
7. http://comedy.clari.net/rhf/jokes/88q1/8028.html

PART 4: YOUR FUTURE

The quality of mercy is not strain'd,
It droppeth as the gentle rain from heaven
Upon the place beneath: it is twice bless'd;
It blesseth him that gives and him that takes:
'Tis mightiest in the mightiest; it becomes
The throned monarch better than his crown;
His scepter shows the force of temporal power,
The attribute to awe and majesty,
Wherein doth sit the dread and fear of kings;
But mercy is above this sceptered sway,
It is enthroned in the hearts of kings,
It is an attribute to God himself,
And earthly power doth then show likest God's
When mercy seasons justice.
Therefore, Jew,
Though justice be thy plea, consider this,
That in the course of justice none of us
Should see salvation: we do pray for mercy,
And that same prayer doth teach us all to render
The deeds of mercy.

—William Shakespeare
The Merchant of Venice, act IV, sc. i, l. 184
(The closing arguments of the defense)

Face it. Going to law school isn't about now, it's all about "later." At this point, you are the "before" picture, with oily skin, hair that wilts, a cheap suit, warts, and bitten fingernails. You jump into the lawyer machine and disappear for a couple years. Once you graduate, you'll expect to be the "after" picture—tall, tailored, pimple free, respected, and rich. Despite what you've been led to believe by the institutionalized, overworked American Dream, education can take you only so far, and then you'd better have some talent or one heck of an inheritance coming. However, the final outcome of your dream is less likely to take on nightmarish proportions if you pick the right law school in the right place. Remember, there are no guarantees. There are Ivy League graduates looking for a dime—two or three, at last count.

> "I don't want a lawyer to tell me what I cannot do; I hire him to tell me how to do what I want to do."
>
> –J. Pierpont Morgan

HIGHEST RATE OF JOB PLACEMENT

Virtually every school has a job placement office on campus, but some are busier than others and some are better than others. If you're going to invest all that time and money, you should have some assurance that you'll get a good job at the end of the ordeal. Twelve percent of all law school grads start their careers as judicial clerks. The most prestigious positions usually go to the nation's elite schools. However, judges have a tendency to hire graduates from their own alma maters (see the list entitled "Graduates on the Supreme Court").

Since the 1990s, over 70 percent of law school graduates go directly into private law firms. The second list under this heading gives you the schools with the best placement record for graduates entering private practice.

Schools with the Highest Clerkship Placement

1. Yale University, Yale Law School
2. Seton Hall University School of Law
3. University of North Dakota
4. Rutgers, The State University of New Jersey School of Law
5. University of Baltimore School of Law
6. Stanford University School of Law
7. Dickinson School of Law
8. Louisiana State University Law Center
9. Northeastern University School of Law
10. University of South Dakota School of Law

Schools with the Highest Private Practice Placement

1. Loyola Marymount University Law School
2. University of Southern California Law Center
3. University of California, Berkeley Boalt Hall School of Law
4. University of California School of Law, Los Angeles
5. Baylor University School of Law
6. Pace University School of Law
7. New York University School of Law
8. University of Louisville School of Law
9. Columbia University School of Law
10. University of Houston Law Center

Let's see: That 12 percent plus 70 percent equals only 82 percent. Do the remaining 18 percent of all law graduates go the way of Amelia Earhart and Jimmy Hoffa? No, that portion of the graduates includes those who go to work for state governments or the Feds, those who take their law degree and go into business or some other line of work than practicing law, those who just take a little longer to find a job ... and a very small percentage who probably do go the way of Earhart and Hoffa. Over 90 percent of graduates from the seven following schools are employed at time of graduation. Six months after graduation, 63 of the 170 law schools have more than 90 percent of their graduates employed. Not bad for a country that already has more lawyers than the rest of the world combined.

Highest Graduate Employment Rate

1.	Columbia University School of Law	92%
2.	Cornell University Law School	90%
3.	Duke University School of Law	97%
3.	Harvard university Law School	97%
5.	Loyola University School of Law, Chicago	92%
6.	New York University School of Law	94%
7.	Yale University Law School	98%

HIGHEST AVERAGE STARTING SALARIES

Most of you are pursuing a law degree in the hope that you can help your fellow men and women. All you really want out of being an attorney is to make the world a better place for truth, justice, and the American way. And if you should, by chance, be paid a premium pile of cash for your services, that will be merely a side effect. However, there are a few of you out there who are just plain venal. For your eyes only, here is the list of the law schools whose graduates have the highest average starting salaries: over $70,000 per year. The rest of you, to prove your good intentions, should go on to the next list without peeking.

1.	Yale University School of Law	$83,000
2.	Columbia University School of Law	$80,000
3.	University of Virginia School of Law	$75,000
4.	Harvard University Law School	$72,000

5. Cornell University Law School	$70,000
5. University of California School of Law, Los Angeles	$70,000
5. University of Pennsylvania Law School	$70,000
5. University of Southern California	$70,000

GRADUATES WHO ARE BESTSELLING AUTHORS

The law is amazingly versatile, multifaceted, and ever-changing. One day you're slaving away in law school, trying to figure out exactly why a tort isn't a dessert treat, and the next minute you're in practice with criminals and entire corporations relying on your skills as a tactician, public speaker, and jurist. Then, before you know it, you've written down everything you know about your clients and your partners in the practice. Bingo! Now you're a bestselling author as well.

The reading public seems particularly insatiable for books about lawyers, their clients (murderers are particularly popular in both fiction and nonfiction), and high profile court cases. If you'd like to be an attorney-writer and rack up some extra vacation money every year, it might help to go to the schools where some of the following literary attorneys got their starts. But since there isn't a clear pattern here, you may have to rely on chutzpah and a little talent.

1. **Alan M. Dershowitz**—Yale University Law School
   Dershowitz is the best-selling author *of Chutzpah, Reversal of Fortune, The Best Defense,* and many more. First in his class at Yale Law School, he was appointed to Harvard's law faculty following two clerkships and became a full professor at 28, the youngest full professor in the school's history. His famous clients include Claus von Bulow, Patricia Hearst, F. Lee Bailey, Michael Milken, and Mike Tyson.

2. **John Grisham**—University of Mississippi School of Law
   His most recent bestseller is *The Partner,* but Grisham is the author of a bevy of bestselling novels, including *A Time to Kill, The Firm,* and *The Pelican Brief.* His books have been made into motion pictures and televi-

sion series. Grisham practiced law for nearly 10 years, concentrating mostly in criminal defense and personal injury litigation. He was also elected to the House of Representatives in 1983 and served until 1990.

3. **Scott Turow**—Harvard University Law School
   A highly experienced criminal defense lawyer and ex-U.S. Attorney who prosecuted corrupt judges and other officials in Chicago's court system, Turow is the author of *Presumed Innocent, The Burden of Proof,* and *Pleading Guilty,* all bestsellers.

4. **David Baldacci**—University of Virginia School of Law
   Baldacci is the new boy on the block, the hot bestselling author of *Absolute Power* and *Total Control.* A sign that he's truly a literary genius on the fast track is the fact that *Absolute Power* has already been made into a big-budget movie starring Clint Eastwood and Gene Hackman.

5. **F. Lee Bailey**—Boston University School of Law
   He may not have managed to write a bestseller, but F. Lee Bailey deserves mention here just because of the amount of ink he's generated over the years. Yes, he's the author of several popular books, including *How to Protect Yourself Against Cops in California and Other Strange Places,* but when one takes into consideration the hundreds of thousands of words that newspapers, magazines, and professional journals have expended on the man, his clients, his cases, and his career—most recently his incarceration for contempt of court for failure to return millions of dollars of reputed drug money—Bailey has probably inspired more writing than any other lawyer in modern history.

6. **Robert L. Shapiro**—Loyola University School of Law
   Mr. Shapiro is fresh in the public consciousness for his participation in the so-called trial of the century, and his book, *The Search for Justice,* detailing his role in the O. J. Simpson criminal trial.

7. **Steve Martini**—University of the Pacific, McGeorge School of Law
   Mr. Martini was a newspaper reporter in Los Angeles who covered the "Helter Skelter" murder trial and became interested in the law watching prosecutor Vincent Bugliosi prosecuting Charles Manson. The law did wonders for his literary career. He is the author of *The Simeon Chamber, Compelling Evidence, Prime Witness, Undue Influence,* and *The Judge.*

8. **Vincent Bugliosi**—University of California Law School Los Angeles
   Bugliosi is the former L.A. prosecutor-turned-author who was the prosecutor in the trial of Charles Manson. He co-authored *Helter Skelter*, a book about Chales Manson's cult of lost souls and the murders they committed at his behest, one of the most chilling and detailed true crime books ever written. Recent events compelled him to pen *Outrage: The Five Reasons Why O. J. Simpson Got Away With Murder*. In this well-reasoned diatribe, he blames Simpson's acquittal on the failings of the prosecution by Marcia Clark and Christopher Darden.

GRADUATES ON THE SUPREME COURT

You had your heart set on appointment to the highest court in the land, the court of last resort, the United States Supreme Court. A lot of people are impressed by all those capital letters, and a seat on that exalted bench would be the crown jewel on your resume if you ever wanted another job. Yet—and it's a shame to have to break it to you this way—there are a few things you should know.

First, you have to be getting on in years before the president will even consider you for the job. And you've probably noticed that the Senate confirmation hearings have become a total drag—if they find out about that ski trip when you mooned the bunny slope from the chair lift, you'll never get the gig. Next, about the only way to get off the Supreme Court is to die. And last, but not least, whether you're a Democrat or a Republican, you almost *have* to be a Harvard graduate to be appointed in the first place. Six of the nine Justices, as well as retired justice Harry A. Blackmun, graduated from Harvard.

1. Breyer, Stephen—graduated Harvard in 1964. He was nominated to the United States Supreme Court by President Clinton in 1994.
2. Ginsburg, Ruth Bader—attended both Harvard and Columbia University School of Law. Nominated to the United States Supreme Court by President Clinton in 1993.
3. Kennedy, Anthony M.—received his LL.B. in 1961 from Harvard. Appointed to the Supreme Court by President Reagan in 1988.

4. O'Connor, Sandra Day—LL.B. in 1952 from Stanford University Law School. Appointed to the bench in 1981 by President Reagan.
5. Rehnquist, William H., Chief Justice—received an LL.B. from Stanford University Law School in 1948. Appointed in 1971 by President Nixon. Became chief justice in 1986.
6. Scalia, Antonin—graduated from Harvard in 1960. Nominated to the United States Supreme Court in 1986 by President Reagan.
7. Souter, David Hackett—a graduate of Harvard University Law School. Appointed to the United States Supreme Court in 1990.
8. Stevens, John Paul—received his law degree from Northwestern University School of Law. Nominated by President Ford in 1975.
9. Thomas, Clarence—graduated from Yale Law School in 1974. President Bush nominated him to the Supreme Court in 1991. He barely made it through the confirmation hearing, when allegations of sexual harassment were made against him by attorney Anita Hill.

GRADUATED MEMBERS OF THE O. J. NIGHTMARE TEAM

Take the leaders of the prosecution, mix them thoroughly with the leaders of the United States basketball Dream Team, and you have a concoction best described as the Nightmare on Main Street that the murder trial of O. J. Simpson became in the minds of American citizens. But they all made a whole lot of money—the defense squeezed their multimillionaire client for every penny they could get, before the civil suit could be pressed to grab O. J.'s fortune. Marcia Clark made millions of dollars on her book deal—and she lost! These folks are definitely on to something, so walking in their footsteps could make your fortune. Here are their alma maters—the names have not been changed to protect the innocent.

Marcia R. Clark received her law degree from Southwestern University School of Law in 1979. Ms. Clark worked for the L.A. District Attorney's office since 1981. After she unsuccessfully prosecuted O.J. in 1995, she received a $4.2 million advance for her book on the trial.

Christopher Darden graduated from University of California, Hastings School of Law in San Francisco. He spent 15 years working in the L.A. District Attorney's office and was an associate professor of law at Southwestern University School of Law in Los Angeles. Mr. Darden had tried 19 murder cases without an acquittal until the Simpson case in 1995, but who remembers those wins?

F. Lee Bailey received his law degree from Boston University School of Law in 1960. He didn't stop shoving himself into the public eye just because the O. J. trial was over. He was jailed in Florida in 1996 for contempt of court for failing to produce $25 million in stock from a drug-dealer client.

Johnnie L. Cochran, Jr., graduated in 1962 from Loyola University School of Law. Mr. Cochran has gone from public service to private practice several times. He worked as a L.A. city attorney from 1963 to 1965, but went into private practice in 1966. Then he returned as an assistant district attorney in Los Angeles County in 1978, only to go back into private practice in 1982. Now that he has his own TV show on Court TV, who knows when we can expect him to practice law again.

Robert L. Shapiro graduated from Loyola University School of Law in 1968. Mr. Shapiro also worked in California's office of the district attorney from 1969–72, and then went into private practice. However, he has not felt the need to return to the employ of the government to ensure a steady paycheck since that time.

WHERE THE LIVING IS EASY

Schools in Areas with the Lowest Cost of Living

Let's say you don't manage to become a Supreme Court Justice, a bestselling lawyer-writer, or a defense attorney for a multimillionaire in big trouble your first year out of law school. Let's say you happened to attend a school with really rotten placement percentages. Even when you get a job, your starting salary is at the low end of the numbers averaged together to get $35,948. Maybe you'd like to own a car, live in a reasonably nice environment, and eat three meals a day most days of the year. You're going to want to be able to stretch those dollars, so it would be a good idea to live where the cost of living is low. If you graduate from a law school in this area, the cost of maintaining life during school will be much lower, perhaps lowering your indebtedness upon graduating. You might also have a better chance of getting and keeping a job, since the local employers will see you as a hometown boy or girl. The government factors in the costs of food, beverage, housing, apparel, transportation, medical care, fuel, utilities, and entertainment in a certain area to come up with the Consumer Price Index. The average for American cities is 148.2. Here are the areas in the United States with the lowest cost of living as measured by the Consumer Price Index and the schools nearby.

1. Tampa–St. Petersburg–Clearwater, FL   126.5
    This is the cheapest place to live in America today, and the sunshine is free. Contrary to popular belief, there are people under the age of 65 living in this area—maybe not in St. Petersburg, but certainly in Tampa.
    Stetson University School of Law, Deland, FL

2. New Orleans, LA   129.0
    The fish are jumping and the cotton is high in the Big Easy. You have to use a machete to cut your way through the summer humidity, and life expectancy is marred by Louisiana's murder rate—the highest per capita rate in the nation—but survival is cheap if you don't weaken. However, fun is readily available, and can cost you plenty in large quantities.
    Tulane University, New Orleans, LA

3. Houston-Galveston-Brazoria, TX   137.9

It's flat, it's humid, and it's industrial. But the Tex-Mex food is great, you can get Lone Star *and* Tecate, the Gulf shore beaches of Padre Island are reasonably close by, the rush hour traffic is truly exciting (the highways are bumper to bumper, but everybody is still going 100 mph), and the price index is right.

University of Houston School of Law, Houston, TX

South Texas College of Law, Houston, TX

Texas Southern University Thrugood Marshall School of Law, Houston, TX

5. Dallas–Fort Worth, TX   141.2

This is the heaven of Texas. If you don't believe it, ask any Dallasite and they will be happy to confirm this information. They have been a little lax with their zoning laws though. It's not unusual to find 35-story high-rise office buildings sprouting up in the middle of suburban tract housing. But this same loose attitude can be a boon if you want to keep your favorite quarter horse in the backyard. There are plenty of neighborhoods in which horses are second only to dogs as pets.

Southern Methodist University School of Law, Dallas

6. Kansas City–St. Louis, MO   141.3

Kansas City has been the central marketplace between the Midwest and the Southwest for hundreds of years. The city rises in steps built on bluffs along the banks of the Kansas and Missouri Rivers. St. Louis is a hub of America's inland waterways with its command of the Mississippi River. The 630-foot high Gateway Arch towers over one of the most successful urban renewal projects in the nation. These are cities of industry, agriculture, and transportation. Think of them this way: Missouri is just California without an ocean.

University of Missouri School of Law, Kansas City, MO

St. Louis University School of Law, St. Louis, MO

Washington University School of Law, St. Louis, MO

7. Cincinnati-Hamilton, OH   142.4

This is a conservative city. They closed down the Robert Mapplethorpe photography exhibition in a heartbeat, and it's almost impossible to find

Playboy magazine on the newsstands here. Maybe you think that's all good. Draped over rolling hills on the banks of the Ohio River, Cincinnati is one of the most scenic towns in the Midwest, plus it's just across the river from Covington and Newport, KY, the wild and wooly towns that play Mr. Hyde to Cincinnati's Dr. Jekyll.

University of Cincinnati School of Law

8. Miami–Fort Lauderdale, FL   143.6
Come so deep South it doesn't even seem southern anymore. What you save on clothes you'll invest in sunscreen to keep those parts of your body that have never seen the sun from getting burned. There are low prices and low wages here, but the Gulfstream and café Cubano make it all worthwhile. You could starve to death in much worse places.

University of Miami School of Law, Miami, FL

St. Thomas University School of Law, Miami, FL

Nova Southeastern University Shepard Broad Law Center, Fort Lauderdale, FL

9. Minneapolis–St. Paul, MN   143.6
Although these cities and the Miami region have the same Consumer Price Index, Minneapolis–St. Paul has snow instead of sunshine and no mountain nearby to offset this disadvantage with skiing, so they drop to Number 9. But Minnesota is the Land of Sky Blue Waters, and the population has set aside more millions of acres for game refuges than any other state. It's also the home of Control Data, 3M, Honeywell, General Mills, Pillsbury, and Land O' Lakes. Don't knock it until you've tried it.

University of Minnesota School of Law

Hamline University School of Law

William Mitchell College of Law

10. Detroit, MI   144.0
There are still blocks in downtown Detroit where you can buy a sagging wreck of an inner city house for less than a used car, but the Motor City is coming back to life after more than ten years of blight and destruction. Backed by a federally financed "empowerment zone" on the site of an abandoned 55-acre Cadillac plant, minority-owned auto part suppliers are providing jobs for a neighborhood that has seen 50 percent unemploy-

ment statistics for many years. Perhaps you can help put the heart back into one of the greatest industrial cities in the world.

University of Detroit School of Law, Mercy

Michigan State University, Detroit College of Law

Wayne State University School of Law, Detroit

NEAR THE JOBS

Schools in Metropolitan Areas with the Highest Projected Growth

If you want your career to take off like a cannonball, then go to school where business is predicted to be booming by the time you graduate. This is a list of the metropolitan areas with the highest projected growth in jobs by the year 2015. Get to where the action is going to be and stay there. It's not a bad idea to pair up the cities that appear both here and on the lowest cost of living list. Here's a hint: Dallas, Houston, Minneapolis, and Tampa.

	New Jobs Expected
Atlanta, GA	1.4 million
Emory University School of Law	
Georgia State University School of Law	
Washington, DC and vicinity	1.3 million
American University Washington College of Law	
Catholic University of America Columbus School of Law	
District of Columbia School of Law	
George Washington University, The National Law Center	
Georgetown University Law Center	
Howard University	
George Mason University School of Law, Arlington, VA	
Los Angeles–Long Beach, CA	1.2 million
Loyola Marymount University, Los Angeles	
Pepperdine University School of Law, Malibu	

Southwestern University, Los Angeles
University of California School of Law, Los Angeles
University of Southern California School of Law, Los Angeles
Whittier College School of Law, Los Angeles

Houston, TX   1.2 million
University of Houston School of Law
South Texas College of Law
Texas Southern University School of Law

Dallas, TX   1.1 million
Southern Methodist University School of Law

Phoenix, AZ   975,000
Arizona State University School of Law, Tempe
University of Arizona School of Law, Tuscon

Seattle, WA   890,000
Seattle University School of Law
University of Washington School of Law, Seattle

San Diego, CA   870,000
University of San Diego School of Law
California Western School of Law

Minneapolis–St. Paul, MN   750,000
University of MinnesotaSchool of Law
William Mitchell College of Law
Hamline University School of Law

Tampa–St. Petersburg–Clearwater, FL   714,000
Stetson University School of Law, Deland

JUST IN CASE

Schools in States that Pay the Highest Average Unemployment Benefits

If there's one thing they teach you in law school, it is to plan for every contingency. You know what they say about the best laid plans of mice and lawyers . . . there you'll be, happily climbing the partnership ladder and working your socks off, when suddenly the whole place goes kablooey because some maniac doesn't like his divorce settlement and blows away half the office with an Uzi. Or your senior partners get caught tampering with the jury. Or you decide to see your first child born instead of billing a thousand hours this week. Worse yet, you might have trouble finding a job in the first place.

Okay, none of this is going to happen to you—but just in case, here are the states that pay the highest average weekly benefits. For your protection, this list is followed by another one that documents the skinflint states that pay the least in unemployment benefits. Move if you have to.

Highest

1. Massachusetts: $217 per week. It's too bad Boston isn't in Florida. This is the kind of money you could live on if you had to.
2. Washington, DC: $213 per week. It's easy for them to pay so much, since everybody works for the government and never loses their jobs. Unemployment in DC just means they have to hire more people to administer the benefits, and they cancel each other out.
3. New Jersey: $207 per week. It doesn't look like much, but as long as you can get your hands on over two hundred a week, you might just make it.
4. Michigan: $204 per week. Hope for an Indian Summer and a mild winter.
5. Connecticut: $201 per week. Maybe it won't pay off your student loan from Yale, but it'll keep you in Ring-Dings until you figure out a new plan.

6. Hawaii: $196 per week. Now we're talking. Assuming you sleep on the beach, you might be able to live on the weekly dole in the islands.
7. Rhode Island: $194 per week. Small state, big stipend, one school.
8. Minnesota: $190 per week. But it all goes to your heating bill.
9. Pennsylvania: $189 per week. They don't pay much for liberty. You'd be better off working.
10. New York: $181 per week. Not bad for a state with more people unemployed than some states have employed. New York pays out close to $2 billion in annual unemployment benefits, trailing only California, which pays an average of $50 less per week.

Lowest

1. Louisiana: $102 per week. Not a good place to get fired unless you like crayfish and know how to catch them.
2. Indiana: $107 per week. Hoosiers evidently do not believe in the free lunch.
3. Mississippi: $111 per week. You'll be living on Mississippi Mud pies.
4. Tennessee: $113 per week. Put your Ford up on blocks and move in.
5. Alabama: $116 per week. Sweat soup isn't too bad.
6. Nebraska: $120 per week. Hope you like corn on the cob. Hope you like cob, for that matter.
7. South Dakota: $120 per week. There's not much unemployment here, but then there's not all that much employment either.
8. California: $131 per week. When the promise leaves the Promised Land, you're on your own.
9. Arkansas: $133 per week. No wonder the Clintons left.
10. Arizona: $135 per week. Take your first check, buy a lizard cookbook, move out into the desert.

ABOUT THE AUTHOR

Mark Baker is the author of eight other nonfiction books published by Simon & Schuster. Two of them, *Nam: The Vietnam War in the Words of the Men and Women Who Fought There* and *Cops: Their Lives in Their Own Words*, are bestsellers. Baker lives in New York City and is currently working on a book about U.S. district attorneys, to be published by Simon & Schuster in spring 1998. His other books include:

Women: American Women in Their Own Words
What Men Really Think
Sex Lives: A Sexual Self-Portrait of America
Bad Guys: America's Most Wanted in Their Own Words
The Insider's Book of Business School Lists
The Insider's Book of Medical School Lists

come to us for the best prep

about KAPLAN

EDUCATIONAL CENTERS

"How can you help me?"
From childhood to adulthood, there are points in life when you need to reach an important goal. Whether you want an academic edge, a high score on a critical test, admission to a competitive college, funding for school, or career success, Kaplan is the best source to help get you there. One of the nation's premier educational companies, Kaplan has already helped millions of students get ahead through our legendary courses and expanding catalog of products and services.

"I have to ace this test!"
The world leader in test preparation, Kaplan will help you get a higher score on standardized tests such as the SSAT and ISEE for secondary school, PSAT, SAT, and ACT for college, the LSAT, MCAT, GMAT, and GRE for graduate school, professional licensing exams for medicine, nursing, dentistry, and accounting, and specialized exams for international students and professionals.

Kaplan's courses are recognized worldwide for their high-quality instruction, state-of-the-art study tools and up-to-date, comprehensive information. Kaplan enrolls more than 150,000 students annually in its live courses at 1,200 locations worldwide.

"How can I pay my way?"
As the price of higher education continues to skyrocket, it's vital to get your share of financial aid and figure out how you're going to pay for school. Kaplan's financial aid resources simplify the often bewildering application process and show you how you can afford to attend the college or graduate school of your choice.

KapLoan, The Kaplan Student Loan Information Program,* helps students get key information and advice about educational loans for college and graduate school. Through an affiliation with one of the nation's largest student loan providers, you can access valuable information and guidance on federally insured parent and student loans. Kaplan directs you to the financing you need to reach your educational goals.

"Can you help me find a good school?"
Through its admissions consulting program, Kaplan offers expert advice on selecting a college, graduate school, or professional school. We can also show you how to maximize your chances of acceptance at the school of your choice.

"But then I have to get a great job!"
Whether you're a student or a grad, we can help you find a job that matches your interests. Kaplan can assist you by providing helpful assessment tests, job and employment data, recruiting services, and expert advice on how to land the right job. Crimson & Brown Associates, a division of Kaplan, is the leading collegiate diversity recruiting firm helping top-tier companies attract hard-to-find candidates.

Kaplan has the tools!
For students of every age, Kaplan offers the best-written, easiest-to-use books. Our growing library of titles includes guides for academic enrichment, test preparation, school selection, admissions, financial aid, and career and life skills.

Kaplan sets the standard for educational software with award-winning, innovative products for building study skills, preparing for entrance exams, choosing and paying for a school, pursuing a career, and more.

Helpful videos demystify college admissions and the SAT by leading the viewer on entertaining and irreverent "road trips" across America. Hitch a ride with Kaplan's Secrets to College Admission and Secrets to SAT Success.

Kaplan offers a variety of services online through sites on the Internet and America Online. Students can access information on achieving academic goals; testing, admissions, and financial aid; careers; fun contests and special promotions; live events; bulletin boards; links to helpful sites; and plenty of downloadable files, games, and software. Kaplan Online is the ultimate student resource.

KAPLAN

KAPLAN

Want more information about our services, products, or the nearest Kaplan educational center?

HERE

Call our nationwide toll-free numbers:

1-800-KAP-TEST

(for information on our live courses, private tutoring and admissions consulting)

1-800-KAP-ITEM

(for information on our products)

1-888-KAP-LOAN*

(for information on student loans)

Connect with us in cyberspace:
On **AOL**, keyword "Kaplan"
On the Internet's World Wide Web, open "http://www.kaplan.com"
Via E-mail, "info@kaplan.com"

Write to:
**Kaplan Educational Centers
888 Seventh Avenue
New York, NY 10106**

Kaplan® is a registered trademark of Kaplan Educational Centers. All rights reserved.
* Kaplan is not a lender and does not participate in determinations of loan eligibility.

A Special Note for International Students

If you are not from the United States and need more help with the complex process of law school admissions and information about the variety of programs available, you may be interested in Kaplan's Access America program.

Kaplan created Access America to assist students and professionals from outside the United States who want to enter the U.S. university system. Access America also has programs for obtaining professional certification in the United States. Here's a brief description of some of the help available through Access America.

The TOEFL Plus Program
At the heart of the Access America program is the intensive TOEFL Plus Academic English program. This comprehensive English course prepares students to achieve a high level of proficiency in English in order to successfully complete an academic degree. The TOEFL Plus course combines personalized instruction with guided self-study to help students gain this proficiency in a short time. Certificates of Achievement in English are awarded to certify each student's level of proficiency.

LSAT (Law School Admissions Test) Preparation
If you plan to enter a law school in the United States, Kaplan will help you determine whether you need to take the LSAT, while helping you to choose an appropriate law program. If you must take the LSAT, Kaplan can help you prepare for it.

Business Accounting/CPA (Certified Public Accounting)
If you are an accountant who would like to be certified to do business in the United States, Kaplan can help you achieve a passing score on the CPA Exam and can assist you in understanding the differences in accounting procedures in the United States.

Applying to Access America
To get more information, or to apply for admission to any of Kaplan's programs for international students or professionals, you can write to us at:

Kaplan Educational Centers
International Admissions Department
888 Seventh Avenue, New York, NY 10106

Or call us at 1-800-522-7770 from within the United States, or 01-212-262-4980 outside the United States. Our fax number is 01-212-957-1654. Our E-mail address is world@kaplan.com. You can also get more information or even apply through the Internet at http://www.kaplan.com/intl.